THE
FORTUNE
RECIPE

THE
FORTUNE
RECIPE

Essential Ingredients
for Creating Your Best Life

BERNIE STOLTZ

HOUNDSTOOTH
PRESS

THE FORTUNE RECIPE
Essential Ingredients for Creating Your Best Life

ISBN   978-1-5445-2842-7   *Hardcover*

       978-1-5445-2843-4   *Ebook*

CONTENTS

FOREWORD

My "Powerful Why" for writing this book is simple. It is my way of paying it forward for the incredible life I have been able to create for myself and my family. My hope is that if even one reader uses the habits, principles, beliefs, and strategies I am sharing to create a better life, then it has served its purpose.

No life is perfect, certainly not mine, but it's possible to believe you can turn your dreams into reality and that life's challenges can be your greatest teacher. My life's journey has included so many wonderful things and experiences I am eternally grateful for. I have a wonderful wife, two great kids, and parents who loved me, and now I get to be a grandpa.

It has also been a journey of experiencing incredible relationships with lifelong friends and business partners—a journey that has allowed me to help create nine companies and travel to numerous countries throughout the world. It has also included rare thrills, from speaking to audiences of five thousand to having a one-on-one lunch with baseball legend Joe DiMaggio at my own restaurant.

Every life experience, whether good or bad, has made this life a glorious journey that I continue to live through the emotions of gratitude, happiness, abundance, and kindness.

This book is written from my perspective as a coach, mentor, CEO, leader, entrepreneur, and person who has chosen to make a difference by helping as many people as possible turn their dreams into reality.

I truly hope this book helps you create your best life.

INTRODUCTION

MY STORY BEGINS BACK IN SAN FRANCISCO, WHERE I WAS BORN to parents who were both nineteen years of age. They were kids, really, who raised me to believe I had to have financial success to be happy. Happiness was defined as being able to do whatever I wanted, whenever I wanted, without concern for money. And so it happened that by the time I was thirty years old, I had already founded five different companies. Back then, most people saw a young guy living the American dream with multiple homes, a beautiful family, and an incredible career.

But today, I say to people, "What if I told you that was maybe one of the scariest times in my life?" I was faced with the reality that if this was all there was to life, I was in trouble. This idea my parents drilled into me about what would create happiness was hollow. I had achieved it all, and I wasn't happy at all. I still had my whole life before me, and frankly, it was terrifying.

At that moment of realization, I made a decision. My life was not going to be about doing whatever I pleased and buying whatever I wanted. It would be about changing my whole focus on personal development. Up until I was thirty, it was all about personal achievement. What became my mantra for living was the process of refining who I was as a person, husband, leader, friend, and citizen. I had to redefine what success really was. I had to redefine how I would find my fortune.

I embarked on a steady process of growth, learning, and personal development, based on helping people achieve their dreams rather than chasing mine. As a result, I have a profoundly fulfilling and satisfying life—and yes, financial wealth too. But my priorities are straight. And along the way, by trial and error and listening, and with my hunger to have greater impact and greater fulfillment, I developed operative principles I could use to guide me as well as guide the other people in my life.

Think of the concepts in this book as a recipe to make a truly successful life. If you want to have a truly rewarding life, those rewards will not always be monetary. In fact, most aren't. When I talk about finding your fortune, I mean finding the most rewarding life you could possibly have with the most success, the most love, the most fulfillment. These guiding principles, lessons, and tools have made it possible for me to have an amazing, purposeful, and fortunate life. These principles may not all apply to you, but I would think twice about discarding any one of them because they don't just work for me—they also work for the hundreds of people I've worked with and coached throughout my career.

As you go through these chapters, you will find that each one ends with a group of powerful questions. I have found that the quality of your life is directly related to the quality of the questions you ask. These questions will help you take action. Finding your fortune is an active process. It won't happen just by reading this book. It's what you *do* with the knowledge that will make all the difference.

Some of these ideas are very practical. Others are subtle but create powerful shifts in mindset. A few are ways of being, and others are ways of being with others. Some are profound, universal truths. Each one will apply to your business, relationships, and community in equal measure. You may apply only one or two of them and find they make a huge contribution to the quality of your life. I suspect the more you do, the more value you'll find.

This is my recipe for a great life, my pathway to finding my fortune. It is a way to be rich in every aspect of your life. And it is my gift to you.

1

ORIGINS

THE FIRST THING I AM GRATEFUL FOR IS MY HUMBLE BEGINNINGS.

When I was ten years old and all my buddies were out playing ball on Saturday mornings, my dad dragged me out of bed and had me work in his gas station, which back then was not just a place where you pumped your own gas like it is nowadays. It was a service station. Back in the '60s, a car pulled in, and a little bell at the pump island rang. Three guys ran out to the car and started pumping the gas, washing the windshield, checking the oil, and checking the air in the tires.

I was the guy who washed all the windows. And they had to be spotless or the customers—or worse, my dad—would complain. When I wasn't doing that, I was vacuuming the cars being serviced or cleaning up the place. I got paid seventy-five cents a day. There were no child labor laws back then.

It may sound like drudgery, but it was one of the greatest gifts my dad ever gave me because it taught me at a very young age about service. I learned how to communicate with adults. It taught me how to speak intelligently. But it also gave me a lot of other things, too, like common sense. Being involved in auto repair and service, you pick up a lot of commonsense rules—even something simple like how to make change for a buck. Most kids today don't even know how to make change or calculate a tip. I learned to do this stuff in my head.

It also taught me about the value of a hard day's work and doing a job right. For example, my dad was a stickler on making sure the bathrooms in the gas station were clean. He had me watch him clean the ladies' room (that's right, it was called the ladies' room back then) to see it done right. Then he told me to do the men's room, after which he would check on me. I didn't have the option to say, "I'm not cleaning toilets for a living." It never even crossed my mind.

It was those types of experiences that instilled a leadership belief I've held my whole life: never ask anyone to do something you aren't willing to do yourself. Leadership by example became my rule. The point I'm trying to make is that I didn't start with anything. As I mentioned, my parents were teenagers when they had me. My dad didn't own the gas station back then. He worked there. And my mom worked in the steno pool at the VA hospital. We lived with my great-grandmother in San Francisco. In reality, she was the only adult in the house. My great-grandmother was my other mother. That's how I grew up.

My parents had no education, no means, and no wealth. Consequently, we didn't have a lot of really nice things. I believe the greatest gifts my parents gave me were good core values and a lot of love. My dad never really caught a break. And so, because that was how life started for me, I knew right away that as soon as I was old enough, I had to do things differently.

It wasn't like I was into education either. I was a bit of a brainiac in elementary school and junior high. I was kind of a nerd: really tall, beanpole skinny, wore glasses. But when I got to high school, I discovered girls and friends and sports. So my grades in high school really fell off. But one of my earliest learning experiences happened when I was a freshman, when the big thing was going out for the football team. Football back then entailed double practice sessions during your summer vacation. So the whole month of August, while everyone else was enjoying their summer, we killed ourselves training.

After two weeks in double sessions, I went home and told my parents, "Look, these coaches are slave drivers. They think they're Napoleon. I'm busting my butt and not getting paid a nickel there. I'd rather work at one of your gas stations and at least get paid."

So the entrepreneurial spirit was present very, very early in my life. I always wanted things like a nice car and money in my pocket, and I learned that hard work could pay off.

This was when all the bakeries in San Francisco were putting out the original sourdough French bread the city was famous for. I knew a guy who said, "You know what? We need baggers to help when the sourdough comes out of the brick ovens and get the bread ready for the trucks to deliver to the restaurants and grocery stores."

When I was seventeen, I got up at four every morning to work this new job. I tell you, the biggest payoff was the smell of that sourdough French bread at five in the morning. I would do that job till about eight o'clock in the morning. Then I'd go to high school. And then after school, I'd go to my dad's gas station, work as the night manager, and do my homework there. The only time during the year I didn't do that was when I played basketball—because I did love basketball.

Because of my jobs, I always had cash. I drove a nice car, could afford gas, and had a few nice things because of my efforts and the work ethic I had at a very young age. My buddies maybe had a great time playing ball and goofing off after school, but they were always beholden to their parents for an allowance. They never had any money, and they drove dilapidated cars and were always scrounging.

I envisioned going to a high-end university as my next step toward success. I'll never forget my junior year when all the college counselors came and visited my school, Westmore High, in Daly City, California.

I came home that night all excited, and I had brochures for some of the schools I wanted to attend, like Stanford, USC, and other cool schools. My dad looked at me and said, "The only way you're going to one of those schools is if you get a scholarship or you find a way to work two or three jobs at the same time because we don't have any money for college."

Truthfully, my parents didn't believe in college. No one in my family had ever gone. They just didn't see it as necessary. They saw work ethic, street smarts, and common sense as necessary, not higher education. Speaking with my dad was a deflating experience. In the end, the only way I was going to college was if I attended the local junior college, paying my own way.

I worked at least two jobs at the same time. It wasn't anything like the fun college experience I had dreamed of. I tried for two years at two different junior colleges. And finally, I just said, "You know what? College isn't for me." Maybe it was the same realization Steve Jobs and Bill Gates had when they quit school, but at least they had prestigious colleges to drop out of.

I decided I could accelerate my path to wealth by getting into the business world at an early age. So at twenty-two years old, I opened my first little tire store in Daly City.

My point in telling you my history is that it doesn't matter where you started. It doesn't matter where you came from. The past never equals the future. Back then, I never dreamed I would be involved in the dental profession, and I had no idea all it would bring to me. I just showed up at my business every day, making my way.

By no means was it a straight path to success and affluence. I learned as much from my failures as my successes. I came to believe that everything happens for a reason. I trusted there was always a lesson, and there were no accidents.

And I was damn hard to stop.

If you don't get a fair break, then you make your breaks. This is America, where so many people's successful journeys start with very little. But I learned that a lot of the things that looked like disadvantages, upon reflection, were advantages that gave me drive, motivation, and street smarts. And one by one, I stacked up guiding principles—rules of the road that came from those experiences.

The big change for me, and this will be true for anyone, is when I found something I truly loved doing. When you love what you do, you'll never work another day in your life because it won't feel like work. For me, I found purposeful work, where I could have a tremendous impact on many people's lives. And that's where Fortune Management came in.

I'll talk about my evolutionary path throughout the book as I present each of my rules of the road. I trust that my story will show you that wherever you are right now, you can get as far as you want to go. Let's begin with the first principle: gratitude.

2

GRATITUDE

My FIRST PRINCIPLE IS GRATITUDE BECAUSE FOR ME, IT'S THE basis for everything in my life. That sense of deep appreciation, the deliberate choice to look for what I have to be grateful for, dominates my behavior. It's even how I start my day.

From a very practical standpoint, I begin each day with a gratitude ritual. Let me first say I've never been a guy who could get into deep meditation. For some reason, it just doesn't work for me. But I practice a daily habit in its place where I get up early because I like to watch the sun come up and make myself a nice espresso. Then I take a few deep breaths, which connects me and grounds me. And then I review my gratitudes.

Let me explain why I do this because I think this practice is one that will help anybody. One of the things I've learned about life is that you get what you look for; you get what you focus on. That starts by asking yourself meaningful questions. Think about it: the whole concept of thought is nothing more than a human being asking and answering their own questions. It flows from the fact that you are your own best audience if you're asking great questions.

So I have learned one of the greatest questions to get your focus is to ask this very powerful, potent question: "What am I most grateful for?"

So I developed my morning gratitude ritual. I do it with a certain cadence. I use my life mastery wheel to look for different gratitudes every day in each of these six areas of my life:

- My emotions

- My health

- My relationships

- My spirituality

- My career

- My lifestyle

I'll come back to this life wheel again and again throughout the book because it really is the foundation for complete life mastery.

EMOTIONAL GRATITUDE

I begin my ritual with what am I grateful for emotionally. I might say I'm grateful that I'm now at a place in my life to be able to choose my attitude. That means I can choose my belief system, and I can choose my core values; I no longer have to buy into somebody else's. I'm grateful I can put myself in a good state of mind.

I've found this leads me to the three emotions I want use as my operating system throughout the course of the day: I want to be happy. I want to be kind to others. I want to see the world as abundant. Gratitude helps me bring those into focus.

When I'm grateful for where my state of mind is, I can use it as a very powerful tool for emotional fitness. It allows me to get into happiness, kindness, and abundance a lot quicker.

Being able to choose your emotions is powerful. And we know that not everyone believes they have the choice. A lot of people believe their attitude or emotions are dictated by whether it's rainy or sunny out, whether they've got a million bucks in the bank, if a special person tells them they love them, or even if it's Monday versus Friday.

In other words, they tell themselves they can't be happy because of *circumstances*. And that's where they go wrong. Think about the pandemic in 2020. How many people bemoaned their situation? Sure, bad things happened. Challenging situations popped up everywhere. But the truth is, I didn't have a bad year. I had a really good year because I looked at the whole experience as a set of blessings to me.

For example, I love to speak in front of others, but I hate airports, and I hate airplanes. Because of the general shutdown, I got a lot of my life back in 2020. It caused me to reassess. I thought about what was most important to me. I think this happened for many people. They reconnected with what was more important to them: health, family, and relationships, as opposed to business success and materialistic gains.

It even caused me to ask, "Where do I want to live? Maybe I don't need to live in a big city anymore. Maybe I don't have to live in Silicon Valley." Again, I think when your mind is open, you've got emotional fitness, and you're willing to ask and honestly answer questions, like "What's really important to me? What isn't?" it can lead you to some real self-discovery.

I ended up moving to a completely different area, and I'm grateful for the change in my lifestyle. I can look back on 2020, ask, "What was great about that year?" and come up with a significant list. Because 2020 didn't "happen" to me. I looked for what was good about it. That's an attitude of gratitude, and it changes how you feel about everything.

When facing any challenge or difficulty, the trick is to ask, "What could be great about this?" That's a great gratitude question. What's the message, lesson, or opportunity in this new obstacle, challenge, or "failure"? This takes away the resentment, despair, and confusion and points you toward a positive outcome.

GRATITUDE FOR HEALTH

The second place I go with gratitude is my health, and I focus on different aspects of it each day. If I had a great night's sleep the night before, I'm grateful for that. I'm grateful that I'm approaching sixty-two years of age and I don't feel like it. I have a great energy level. I'm grateful every time I get a workout in. I'm grateful every time I ride my bike. I'm grateful every time I get out and play a round of golf. I'm also grateful when I eat a good, healthy meal. I'm grateful for different little things in the area of health.

GRATITUDE FOR RELATIONSHIPS

Then I go to the third part of the wheel: relationships. I think the most powerful question here is, "Who do I love, and who loves me?" I think about all the wonderful, loving people that are in my life, starting with my wife and the forty-year relationship we've had.

Then I go outward to my children and my grandson. Then I expand to the friends I have. I had a large group of friends, and we all got together when we were in junior high—so literally fifty years ago. There are maybe a dozen of us left now, and I am so grateful for them because friendships should never be taken for granted. I'm grateful for other individuals in my family, but I'm particularly grateful for the friendships I get to choose.

I am grateful for the relationships I have within our company. At this point, we now have about 120 advisors, and it bothers me when I'm not in a good place with any one of them. I am deeply grateful for having great, great relationships at work.

In this profession of coaching and advising, you become great friends with your clients. When they hurt, you hurt. And when they win, you win. I'm grateful for all of them and grateful that I get to work with a high-quality group of professionals with strong core values.

I'm also grateful for all I've learned about how to make relationships work. For example, one of the things I say in live seminars is that *relationships are where you give, not where you get.* Whether it be in a work environment, in a business relationship, in a family, or with a love interest, whoever it is, just look to give. I have a career where I get to help people, and the people I help also have careers that are about helping people. It's deeply gratifying.

This ties directly into the law of attraction, which I'll talk more about later. This choice of leading with a giving hand has attracted amazing people to me. And of course, nothing makes relationships work better than expressing gratitude.

I know that it's easy for you as a reader to say, "Oh, well, of course he's grateful. Look at the life he lives now." But that's not the secret. The secret is to be grateful when you *don't* have much of anything. When I was thirty, I learned to be grateful when I had just lost a million dollars. I needed to find things to be grateful for, otherwise I was going to wallow in self-pity and resentment. That never would have gotten me out of that hole. If you can ask "What's great about this?" when you don't have success, when you have challenges, or even when you have disasters, and you don't give up until you have real answers, then nothing can hold you back.

When I walk into a seminar room, I tell my audience the first thing we need to do is get grateful. And I mean grateful for the little things. Be grateful your heart never misses a beat, 100,000 times a day. Be grateful for the way your body works. Be grateful for the time and the place we live today, which is the greatest time and place ever to be alive.

As usual, there will be people who argue about that last one. My dad is one of those people. How many older folks want to talk about the "good old days"? I always have to remind him, "You mean the good old days when we died younger, had unchecked diseases, and had way less access to knowledge, convenience, and safety?" People can now fly in an airplane at 30,000 feet and get to a destination in five hours that used to take five days by train or five months by wagon, and yet people get very upset because the Wi-Fi doesn't work at Starbucks.

I've seen that people who are reactive and let negative emotions dominate usually are not grateful. And they're also not happy. So I remind people of these very potent facts: you can't be angry and grateful at the same time. You can't be resentful and grateful at the same time. You can't be hateful and grateful at the same time. This is how gratitude can alter your perspective. You can shift your reaction from one negative thing to ten positive things in an instant.

Finally, it's important to note we won't always have these relationships. They are all finite, as are we. As abundant as my life is, nothing shielded me from losing my best friend to cancer four years ago. Despite the deep sorrow, I can be grateful for fifty years of joyful times together. As I mined that loss even deeper, it resulted in a clear decision to never leave anything on the table. I'm going to buy that Ferrari. I'm going to spend two weeks in Italy every year. I'm going to eat that piece of cake. Whatever adds joy and meaning to my life, I'm going to do it. Not someday but now.

SPIRITUAL GRATITUDE

The fourth area of life mastery is what I term spirituality. You can call it religion, faith, integrity, or your connection to the universe.

Personally, I'm not a religious guy. I was raised in a strict faith, and at some point in my adult life, I just decided there were a lot of things in the religious doctrines I didn't agree with. I couldn't condone the judgment. I couldn't buy into the concept of sin. There were certain things I didn't see as positive, as truly Christian. To me, there is a huge difference between being religious and being spiritual because people today are still killing one another in the name of religion around the world. And that's not very spiritual.

I view spirituality as something different. It's about the power of my intention. For me, that intention is about giving and giving back, about making the world a better place. Along with that, it means being the best person I can be, acting with integrity, and keeping my promises.

My daily spiritual gratitude is about the opportunity to give and to help as many people as possible. Another way to put it is to ask yourself, "Who am I serving today?" I will go into this in more detail later when we discuss spirituality as a principle, but there is nothing wrong with doing well and succeeding financially by doing good things for other people.

When it comes to relationships, you want to be grateful anytime you have the ability to contribute value to someone else's life. That's the dream scenario in my mind, where all the little concerns in life drop away. My heart swells with gratitude when I'm able to do that.

My gratitudes in this area are always about who I was able to help and whose life I made a difference in. It sets my intention to do more of that.

GRATITUDE FOR CAREER

The fifth area of Gratitude is my career. And with this there is always one constant: the fact I get to do something I love. I'm so grateful for the opportunity to do it. I'm grateful I've been able to create multiple streams of revenue by creating multiple companies and entities. I'm grateful to have built purposeful companies that are all about serving, helping, and making people their best selves.

And one more thing. If you believe you can be grateful by helping others and giving more than you get, then you're also believing in the positivity and support of the universe. I believe the good you do always comes back to you in one form or another, and that belief has never failed me.

GRATITUDE FOR LIFESTYLE

And then there is the sixth area of life mastery, which is lifestyle. When I was younger, I chased more financial goals, and then I was grateful for financial freedom—for having more than enough money. Even before I reached that level, I was grateful because I believed it was coming.

Today, I've shifted my gratitude beyond financial freedom to being grateful for what it has given me, which is my lifestyle. So when I coach people now, I help them make a shift to gratitude as they process their success. When you're younger, you chase financial goals and materialistic gains. But once you get there, gratitude has to be even more important. Say to yourself, "Look at the lifestyle I get to live," and really decide what is important. It's a time to question how much more financial success you really need and what you might end up giving up in lifestyle to get it.

When I read Ray Dalio's book *Principles,* it struck me when he said that in reality, being a billionaire versus being someone who has financial freedom is not that different. I think we put too much emphasis on the title "billionaire" today. Quite frankly, they don't live any better than I do. Sure, they might fly in more private jets, and they might drink a more expensive bottle of wine and have more homes, but they might also have a few things I don't care for.

I don't measure my life by my portfolio; I measure it by my lifestyle.

I don't want to own a $20 million yacht. I can go on a cruise whenever I want. I don't want five servants in my house all the time. I don't want to live in a walled compound with twenty-four-hour security.

You can only sleep in one bed at a time, and you can only eat so many meals a day. You can overindulge yourself but soon discover it doesn't make you happy. Chasing status becomes a hollow goal. My belief right now is that I live as good a lifestyle as any billionaire on the planet. And that's for two reasons: I'm grateful for all I have, and I'm not measuring myself by my portfolio. I'm looking at my lifestyle.

So you have to ask, "What's the end game?" If you created enough wealth to do whatever you want, as much as you want, for as long as you want, with whomever you want for the rest of your life, why would you sacrifice your time and energy to make five or ten times more money? You have to decide for yourself what's important. The lifestyle you want may only require $10 million in the bank. Or it may require $100 million. I guarantee it won't require a billion dollars. My point is, don't get so wrapped up in the money you lose sight of why you're doing what you're doing.

No matter where you are in your career or how close you are to financial freedom, if you are grateful every step of the way for the lessons, relationships, and opportunities to contribute to other people's lives, the money will always be enough.

SUMMARY

So that's how I start my day. The specific gratitudes can change day to day based on the moment or based on where my focus is on a particular day, but I always begin from this place of gratitude. It's about resetting your focus, priming your attitude. Because you get what you get in life—the good, the bad, and the ugly—and it's different for everyone. But what matters is how you react to it and what you discover you are grateful for, no matter the loss, hardship, or challenge. Then you're always winning and, I believe, truly happy.

POWERFUL QUESTIONS:

- What am I grateful for?

- What is most important to me in life?

- What does wealth really equate to in my life?

- What is the lifestyle I want?

- Who am I serving today?

3

HUNGER, PASSION, AND ENERGY

Hunger, passion, and energy are deeply intertwined and interdependent, so I'm bundling them together as a single concept for you here.

People often get confused about the concept of hunger. They think that in order to be hungry, to feel that deep inner drive to achieve something, you have to be in scarcity or avoiding pain—that's what creates hunger. I remind people that a guy like Warren Buffett is just as hungry to do a deal or make an investment in a new company today as he was fifty years ago. Michael Iger, the CEO of Disney for many years, didn't just stop when he bought Marvel. He then acquired Lucasfilms, Pixar, and Fox Films.

I could give you a hundred more examples of hungry people at every level of success. Hunger has nothing to do with scarcity. Hunger, passion, and energy all keep you in what I call a proactive state. Hunger can lead you to your passion, or your passion could make you hungry, and both will increase your energy. Then, all three synergistically propel each other.

For me, hunger drove me to be successful as a young man and gave me a level of passion, but then I hungered for something more fulfilling. Though the hunger gave me energy, it wasn't enough until I found Fortune Management, and my passion was fully ignited. And it still is.

Every day I'm hungry for that next opportunity to have an impact on someone, improve a division, or add a service. I'm not hungry in terms of a desperate need to succeed, but I'm still driven because the passion is there.

In talking about how I found my fortune, I look back and realize that whatever I've done at any stage in my life, I have always done it with passion. Maybe it's because I'm Italian. Italians tend to be passionate, loving people, so maybe it's a little bit of that. But I just know that passion makes you more believable and makes your ideas more credible. The opposite is also true. If you have a brilliant product or an innovative service but you don't present it with passion, people won't be interested.

Let me add a warning to this: don't make your passion just about making more money. Money should be the *result* of your passion and energy. It should be a byproduct, not a purpose. My experience has been that when money is your primary driver, people can smell it on you. It smells like desperation.

When you're motivated by money, people can feel the lack of integrity, the lack of caring about them as the end user. They can sense that as long as you are the one winning, it's okay if they come up short in the deal. This may work for you in the short term and get you a few bucks, but I can tell you that nothing is hollower in the end. Make your passion about *everyone* winning, and that will last a lifetime.

Your passion should also drive you to make yourself and your business better, especially for the end user. When that happens, you build a virtuous cycle. When a customer truly benefits, it feeds your passion and gives you energy, making you hungry to do even more for them.

If you look at people who've done anything of magnitude, they're passionate about it. They leap out of bed in the morning to do it. It seems like they can't be stopped. People line up behind them to support them. When you are truly passionate about your business, you inspire people and attract people to that passion.

For real success, passion has to be there. You've got to be excited at your core. This doesn't mean you're bouncing around shouting from the rooftops all the time—passion can be quiet. The intensity can be right below the surface. You can be calm and passionate. But passion creates emotion, moving you beyond just an intellectual process. You don't *think* passion; you *feel* it. The more passionately you feel about a romantic interest, a cause you believe in, or a business you want to create, the more powerful your hunger, and the more energy you derive from it.

When people are passionate about what they are doing, they don't worry about how much time it takes or how hard it is. They are in it completely, and that passion and hunger create all the energy they need to achieve it. This type of energy is the fuel of excellence.

There are two types of energy. There's the kind you get from physical workouts and sports, and being healthy. But then there is the energy that comes from passion. When you're passionate about a new love, a new event, or a new initiative in your business, you can feel the energy pouring through you. It seems boundless. And it is. It's what propels you toward excellence, to be unsatisfied with "just good enough." Once again, achieving excellence fuels your passion. It's a constant positive feedback loop.

WEALTH IS SECONDARY

In my late twenties, I was seeking to move beyond just commercial success, and I was inspired by Napoleon Hill's classic book, *Think and Grow Rich.* Of course, the title sounds like it's about making money, but if you really read the book, it's about how you live your life. In many ways, that's what this book is about as well. As I said in the introduction, your true fortune will not likely be money, even though pursuing your passion and purpose will often generate all the wealth you will ever need.

But the reality of it is the wealth is secondary. What comes first is how you live your life. I've always lived my life with passion and energy. And because of that, it's driven my hunger, my burning desire. Napoleon Hill talks about a burning desire. I think if you were to interview a hundred people who have made a real difference in the world, the one commonality will be their burning desire.

Throughout this book, I'm going to be asking powerful questions. This applies to questions you ask yourself just as much as those you would ask someone else. As your hunger and passion emerge, the big question becomes, "What is my promise?" You need to dig deep and articulate for yourself the promises you make in business and every aspect of your life. And let's remember what a promise is: it's something that hasn't happened yet. A promise is about the future.

A promise is somewhat like a goal. The only difference is that a promise is also a commitment. It's putting your butt on the line, which is another one of my success secrets. When you make a commitment, you are declaring something will happen, no matter what. A goal may or may not be achieved based on many factors. A promise, if made in earnest and with integrity, *must* happen. It must be fulfilled.

You are either living your promises or you are a victim.

Ask yourself what you want to be said about you in your eulogy. That in turn becomes a promise you must make to yourself daily: to be that person. You may also ask yourself, "What is my promise to my career? What is my promise to my team? What is my promise to my marriage? What's my promise to my body?"

One of the things successful people do is always hold their promises mentally in a place where they're really, really important because they've had this transformational insight that they are either living their promises or they're the victim. If you're not living your promises, you're abdicating control of your life and your behavior. You're saying you don't have a choice, but you know you do. That negative thinking will kill your passion, hunger, and energy.

It's important to understand that sometimes what you're passionate about doesn't have anything to do with money or even business success. You may be most passionate about being a great parent and providing opportunities for your children to have good lives. If your job provides the income you need for that goal, then you can be passionate about any career, even if it's not directly linked to your passion, because it supports your *true* passion. That true passion gives you the hunger and energy to excel at your job.

In this case, your fortune is your family. And there's certainly nothing wrong with that. But some people lose sight of that, and say, "My job is pointless. I don't care about it." And that drains your energy. There is no hunger, except to escape. And that's because you haven't asked yourself what matters, what's important, and what's great about what your job gives you. I know people whose greatest passion is surfing, and they wait tables so they can always have the freedom to surf. And they are happy waiters—energetic and positive. They do a great job because their passion is being supported.

Your passion is your promise to yourself to give your life the meaning that matters most to you. And hopefully you will find you can approach everything that matters in life with passion. It won't be just one thing. Why not be passionate about your marriage, health, faith, and career?

I'll keep coming back to this concept of making promises. How strong are your promises? Are you passionate about them? Are you willing to put your integrity on the line for them? Because if you are, you will always be hungry to do better, and the energy will always come.

POWERFUL QUESTIONS

- What is my true passion—my burning desire?

- How strong are my promises in each area of my life?

4

WORK AND SPEAK FROM INTENTION

THE LESSON HERE IS SIMPLE. WHEN YOU ARE IN PURSUIT OF your passion, you must have a clear intention behind what you say and do with your time. If you aren't working with a clear intention, you shouldn't be surprised at a meager result. If you are talking just to converse, don't be surprised if there is no outcome at the end. Always have an intention with every action when you are acting in pursuit of your goal. Your passion and your energy are wasted without it.

This requires a conscious effort to check yourself right at the outset and determine what exactly you hope to achieve by the call or the undertaking. This sets a direction. Without that, how could you expect to reach a desired outcome? Think of it as heading toward a lighthouse. Your outcome could be a sale closed, a deal made, or a solution or insight provided to another person.

It's very easy to fall into the trap of activity as the desired result in and of itself. For example, a salesperson could have the goal of making a hundred cold calls every day. And that's a good start, but if the salesperson is satisfied with that even if they didn't make any sales, then that indicates intention was missing. They made activity the goal. They didn't set their true intention, which was to make sales.

Your passion and hunger will give you energy, but it won't be infinite. You'll actually lose energy faster if you are in the activity trap because hunger and passion are fed by achievement. Sometimes activity feels like you're achieving something in the moment, but you're fooling yourself, and you're burning fuel.

Without a clear intention, your passion and energy are wasted.

This also means you have to be careful about the people in your business and in your life who are time-wasters. Beware because there are a lot of people roaming the earth who speak simply because they have air. They are happy to gobble up your time, and suddenly the clock runs out on your day. It doesn't matter to them because they had no intention. They just wanted attention. Don't be one of those people. When your interaction has intention, there is an outcome, and people will learn to appreciate that about you.

THE IMPORTANCE OF LISTENING

You want to keep refining the life skill of intention. One of the things I learned when I came into dentistry was taught to me by the late Dr. Omer Reed. He was a master of succinct statements. He said, "If you want to speak, first listen." I've heard this put another way, which is this axiom: I've never learned anything by speaking, only by listening.

This is where speaking with intention comes in. Listen with the intent to understand, not to reply. I can't emphasize enough how important this behavioral adjustment is. We're all guilty of this mistake. How many times are we in a conversation, and we can't wait for the other person to stop speaking so we can start talking? That's not good intention. The ideal intention would be to really understand what the other person is saying and learn from it so when you do speak, you're speaking to their real challenge.

Here's something else to remember when you think you are speaking with intention but you haven't been truly listening: until it can come out of the other person's mouth, it's not true for them. They didn't get it. You may have been heard, but they weren't persuaded. Maybe they didn't even understand.

Asking Questions

The easiest way to trigger your listening is by asking questions. Once again, it comes down to the quality of those questions. By way of example, when we get a new client at Fortune Management, the initial conversation always includes these five questions:

1. Where are you right now?

2. How did you get here?

3. Where do you want to go?

4. Do you have a plan to get yourself there?

5. How can I help?

Now, let me elaborate on each of these questions.

1. Where are you right now?

That's a loaded question, isn't it? I could be asking about their life, career, relationships, or any other area of their life. It's deliberately open-ended. But by waiting to see which area they respond about first, I discover what's most important, or possibly a pain point. This gives me a place to start. My intention with the question is simple: to discover how they see themselves. I am listening to understand.

2. How did you get here?

This elicits the history that led to their situation. It may be a success story or a nightmare, and they will tell you what they perceive to be the causes. It doesn't matter if you agree with them. You're just finding out how they believe they got there. You find out which promises were made and kept and which ones were broken.

3. Where do you want to go?

You've set up point A, where they are, and now this is point B, where they want to be. You cannot guess this on your own or make assumptions. They have to tell you. And that will create the promises you both will make. Your intention is to find out if they're clear on where they want to go and how committed they are to achieving that goal.

4. Do you have a plan to get yourself there?

This is where the pain often comes in. They have a sense of where they want to be, but they can't figure out the steps to get there. It forces them to acknowledge their lack of strategy, lack of capability, and more.

5. How can I help?

You may already have a clear sense of what you can offer them, but that doesn't matter yet. Your intention is to find out what they need from you or what they believe you can provide.

Do you see how every one of those questions allows them to tell me their own truths? Do you understand how powerful listening to the answers can be? This specific set of questions may not apply to your situation or business, but the process and deliberate nature of the questions applies to everything you want to do with intention.

TIME MANAGEMENT

Here's a quick thought about time management. I think it's become a buzzword that is completely fallacious. You can't manage time. It runs at the same speed for everyone. What you are managing is your energy, and you maximize that energy by speaking and working with intention.

When I end my morning gratitudes ritual, I always ask these powerful questions: "Where will I invest my energy today? What will provide the most value for me and others in the shortest amount of time?"

By asking those questions, I'm setting an intention for how I'm going to work right at the outset. It will influence every part of my day, and I will maximize my energy during the next few hours life has given me.

POWERFUL QUESTIONS:

- Do I speak and engage with a clear intention in mind?

- Who wastes my time?

- Do I listen to understand?

- Where will I invest my energy today?

5

APPRECIATE BUSINESS

A KEY PART OF BEING SUCCESSFUL IN BUSINESS IS TO REALLY appreciate what business does, how it impacts the world, and what it achieves. You'll often hear people dismiss business as less noble than, say, working for some charity, trying to save the world, or creating beautiful art. But that misunderstands business. I believe business goes way beyond commerce and capitalism—it's something much more profound.

I'm not the most creative guy in the world, artistically speaking. But I've always been an innovator. I've always been someone who, if I saw something good, felt I could make it better. One thing that's always been cool in my eyes—and I deliberately use the word *cool*—is creating and refining a business, an enterprise that will do so much for so many people.

A great business serves many different functions. First of all, it serves the consumer. In other words, whatever that business provides makes somebody's life better in some big or small way.

Business also has a cascading effect. It creates jobs. Then, people spend their earnings, which grows the economy. It generates more in taxes, so we have better roads and bridges and schools and support systems. And the best businesses give their people a sense of purpose, a sense of achievement, a way to better themselves and be the most they can be.

Businesses allows people to pursue their passions. Not just the owners, but the people who are passionate about their careers. They provide good incomes for others so they can pursue their true passions, which may not generate a lot of money but feed their souls. How is that not a good thing?

The best businesses give their people a sense of purpose.

Not everyone has a strong purpose for their life. Some just want to live comfortably. But businesses make that possible too. People get to show up, meet a need of the business, and even if they don't always acknowledge it to themselves, there is a satisfaction in that.

The value of the business's founders being passionate about their business works its way down to everyone on the team. One of the things I'm most proud of with Fortune Management is how grateful people are to carry a Fortune business card because they believe it means something.

There's a purposeful existence for those involved with our company. I think it gives people passion. And, of course, it gives them income so they can go out and do good things for their families and themselves to enhance their lifestyle. I find it interesting that not everybody appreciates business. There's currently a great deal of negativity about capitalism, and I realize capitalism at its best is pure competition. Competition creates winners and losers, and many people are opposed to that competition. They value enforced equality over freedom of competition, but no system is perfect. I just happen to believe that our capitalist system has built the best and most generous economy the world has ever known.

There are bad players in every arena, but the majority of businesses have to create real value and good jobs or they will go under. It's an economic fact. The more purposeful your business and the more refined your business culture, the greater your opportunity to create a legacy for yourself and reward the people who dedicate themselves to your business success.

Are you doing it in part to make money? Of course. But there's nothing wrong with that. This leads us to my next principle: Do Well by Doing Good.

POWERFUL QUESTIONS:

- Do I truly appreciate what business contributes to the world?

- Do my team members value their contribution?

6

DOING WELL
BY DOING GOOD

LET'S TALK ABOUT BEING WEALTHY. THERE IS A WIDESPREAD misconception that making a lot of money is inherently a bad thing. It assumes that because one person became financially successful, someone else lost out. That assumes a zero-sum game, which is proven to be an absurd notion, given the American economy has grown steadily for over three centuries. This misconception also comes from a scarcity mindset. More about that later.

The healthier belief is that it is okay to do well by doing good. There is absolutely nothing wrong with financial success derived from a business that benefits its customers.

In fact, that's kind of the point. For a business to sustain itself, it has to be profitable. Capitalism has a Darwinian aspect to it. So why should it be that the person who has the idea, puts in the most time, and takes the most risk should not be successful? In my mind, they should be wildly successful, which means the business will go on for many years, creating value for customers, creating more jobs, and contributing to the community in myriad ways.

Certainly, there will always be bad players and businesses that do more damage than good. To that I say, don't be a bad player. Don't create that kind of business. Don't pursue that kind of career. But don't judge someone simply by their wealth, and don't create a limiting belief that if you are wealthy, you're automatically taking advantage of people.

Free yourself from a limiting belief about financial success.

That's an important point. I know many people who limit their own success or beat themselves up when they do better than other people, despite the fact they have a great product and dedicated employees. They've bought into the false notion they don't have the right to do better financially than others.

That's bullshit.

When you think that way, you are out of alignment. Your behavior is incongruent, and it's going to hold you back. You have a deep limiting belief that your success and reward for it make you a bad person. Sometimes this is subconscious, and you sabotage your success. Take a hard look at yourself and see if you have this mindset. If you do, find out where it came from, and then ask yourself how it could possibly be true.

Everything I've talked about so far, from gratitude to passion, energy, and hunger, leads you to doing well (hopefully really well) by doing good things for the marketplace. One of the rewards for that is financial. It's not the only one but certainly an essential one.

When you're contributing to others in your career path—and, even more, if you can control your career path by creating a business—you're serving three key human needs: the need for significance, the need for growth, and the need for contribution. These are high-level needs, and they lead to a truly fulfilling life. When you put your energy into building something, push yourself to learn and grow, and serve others as a result, you've unlocked the secret to a happy life.

In my experience, this is also the difference between a good business and a great business. I had already accomplished a lot financially by age thirty, but I had a destructive personality. I wasn't a good person. I was making a lot of money because I was told at an early age it would make me happy, and my only purpose in business was to make more of it. The customers didn't lose out because they were good, solid businesses. But they didn't fulfill me, so I indulged myself.

In doing this, I put myself into this artificial euphoria. I had to spend money to make myself happy because I wasn't making money for the right reasons. And, hey, I was young. My financial success came perhaps too early, and when I was eventually forced to take a hard look at myself, I realized I needed growth and real significance from a higher purpose and greater contribution. So now, years later, I am proud of what I've built and who I've become because financial success is merely a byproduct, not my purpose. *That's* truly great business.

In the end, the only question you need to ask is, "Does everybody win?" Then go make millions or even billions. The amount of money you make at that point is an indicator of how much good you're doing in the world and in people's lives and how much you're advancing the economy. You are undoubtedly creating wealth for your own employees as well. It's misguided—even dumb—to beat yourself up over that. And it's even dumber for people to judge you for that or for you to buy into their judgment.

Also, how can you be generous in a significant way or support charities you believe in if you are not financially successful? Look at the worldwide impact the Bill and Melinda Gates Foundation has, as well as many others like it. Some may call Americans greedy and capitalistic, but the reality is that we donate a greater percentage of our income than any other country in the world.

The more you gain, the more you can give away. It's not a complicated formula.

Build something good. Make people's lives better. And for God's sake, relax and enjoy the fruits of your labor. It's absolutely okay to do well by doing good.

POWERFUL QUESTIONS:

- What do I believe about wealth?

- Who benefits from my career or my business?

- Are there people in my life who have limiting beliefs about financial success?

7

DEFINING SUCCESS

I HAVE A VERY SIMPLE FORMULA FOR ACHIEVING SUCCESS: find out what other people want, and then fill that need quickly and elegantly. What does that mean?

In its purest form, it means you should view every relationship as an opportunity to give, not to get. If you can take this guiding principle into the business world, you can't help but thrive.

This mindset is part of what creates great culture in an organization. But I think it also creates a great lifestyle. And there is another dimension to this, which is a concept I have taught in case presentations and enrollment skills for years, and that is to be keenly aware of the fact that it doesn't matter what you think the benefit is for the consumer. The only thing that matters is what the consumer *wants*.

Very often, I see people with a product or service, and they have decided what the most important features are, so that's what they present. They skip the first step of the formula, which is finding out what that specific customer wants. So a great product crashes on the hard rocks of a marketplace that doesn't see its value.

This is not the marketplace's fault. It's yours. You may have a way to fill certain needs quickly and elegantly for your customer, but you haven't isolated their *specific* need yet. By determining what matters to the customer, you can build upon that and find more customers who have that same need. You may think the most brilliant part of your service is the marvelous dashboard you've created, but all the customer cares about is that the software does what they need without them having to look at anything, including a dashboard. So you missed the mark. And the sale.

All that matters is what the customer wants.

As always, it comes down to asking the right questions. You need to ask, "What's most important to you, the customer?" In my businesses we actually label them *WMIs*. We don't assume anything. We find out their WMIs, and in their order of priority. We need to know: is it price? Reliability? Ease of use? Trustworthiness of the company? Or does twenty-four-hour customer service response matter most? How can we know without asking?

Then it's essential to probe even deeper and find out *why* those are the priorities. Maybe they've been burned by another company, or they want something simple enough to delegate to someone else so it doesn't take up their time.

I think most business Success comes from building relation-
ships with customers, so let me use a first date as an example.
Let's say you are out to dinner with a potential love interest.
A really cool question to ask over the first cocktail might be,
"What's most important for you in life?"

What you're doing is eliciting their core values. They might
say, "The most important things to me in life are freedom,
adventure, and trust." They could express a dozen core values
or more. Draw those things out.

The next part is critical. There are really two things you are
trying to elicit, and this applies to sales situations and relationships of any type. You want to understand their values,
but then you want to know their *rules* about those values.
Those rules delineate what has to happen in order for that
person to get what's most important for them.

Let's continue the dating analogy. This could apply to any
gender in any new relationship, but let's say you're a man,
and you go out with two different women. You ask them the
exact same question: "What's important to make you feel
loved?"

They both give you the exact same answer. Each one says love,
passion, and compatibility are most important. But you then
ask the second question, which is, "What has to happen for
you to feel truly loved by someone?"

The first one responds, "I need someone who is emotionally
available, who listens and is there when I need him." These
are her rules about a healthy, loving relationship.

You ask the second woman her rules, and she explains, "I need to eat in the best restaurants, and I need a new BMW every couple of years. I need a new wardrobe with every change of season. If a man does those things for me, along with a couple of trips to Europe every year, I know he loves me."

Same answer to the first question, but entirely different responses for the second one. If you don't ask the second question, you start to make assumptions. And you could be off by 180 degrees. First seek to understand, and then you will know how to fill that need. Or you may decide you don't even want to.

By the way, when you're asking these kinds of questions, the person on the other end feels like you really want to get to know them. By showing a true interest in what's important to them, you honor their individuality.

This goes right back to Appreciating Business and Doing Well by Doing Good. If you're in a business and your intent is to find out what people really want, and then fill the need quickly and elegantly, that's a good thing. That's something the customer truly appreciates. You know you're doing good for them because they've told you what's important and how to deliver it.

Imagine if we approached every business relationship this way. How powerful would that be? It would build word-of-mouth advertising and loyalty and even create a feedback loop. If you're smart enough to implement it, you can find out when you aren't filling their needs in the way they want. That's good business. In fact, that's great business.

This can apply to every aspect of your life. Why wouldn't you want to know what is important to your life partner, children, or employees and how to give that to them?

To me, it comes down to this: to succeed in business, you have to know how you make other people feel. This can only happen when you truly understand what they want and devote yourself to continuously filling those needs as quickly and elegantly as possible.

POWERFUL QUESTIONS:

- Do I understand other people's values and rules?

- Does my business fill actual needs quickly and elegantly?

8

NO WORK, NO PLAY, JUST LIFE

I HEAR WAY TOO MANY PEOPLE EXPOUNDING ON THE IDEA OF work-life balance, with pundits preaching compartmentalization of your daily life. They advise things like at precisely five o'clock, you should shut work off completely and then get to the other parts of your life. But the way many people are working today, especially entrepreneurs, that concept doesn't apply at all.

Building on my previous principles, the ideal that can emerge in your life is that there is no sharp division between and work and play. You are just living your life to the fullest. You are constantly blurring that line because your "work" is play, with people you love, and there is no need to shut work off every day.

It's also not practical.

By way of example, it certainly doesn't make sense for the people in my company to stop working at five o'clock. If you're going to be an executive coach, then you'll be doing evening and possibly weekend calls, and you need to be available when it's convenient for your clients.

This doesn't mean you are a slave to your career and it supersedes everything in your personal life. I think you have to be the architect of your entire life, with the goal of having complete freedom to do *what you should be doing with your time.* That may seem to be a contradiction, but when put into action, based on things you are truly passionate about, it means you're using all your time effectively and purposefully in pursuit of your dreams. Those dreams can include your health, sports activities, family, community, and career. By design and intention, they can all blend together.

This is a cornerstone concept when it comes to finding your fortune. Creating a life that is rich in all aspects requires a deliberate approach to integrate all of your activities. Sir Richard Branson, the billionaire creator of the Virgin empire, could certainly spend all his time playing. Instead, he is constantly diving deep into new enterprises—cruise lines, space travel, rapid train systems—and having a great amount of fun doing it. But he's not a workaholic. He plays tennis, windsurfs, and is a dedicated family man.

It isn't that he found a balance. He just eliminated separate definitions. It's how he lives. And I've designed the same approach to life. I don't think there are many successful people who shut their work off every day at five. They can't, but they also don't need to. They are living their passion. They are not punching a time clock with their purpose.

If you're going down an entrepreneurial path, you will blur those lines all the time. This conversation of compartmentalizing your life is pointless for someone who's passionate about their pursuits. There's an adage that says to find something you love to do, and you'll never work another day in your life. Words to live by.

If we pursue this elusive thing called work-life balance, we are trapping ourselves with definitions. I just want to live a big life. I love what I do, and I love the people I do it with. I think you can make work fun. First of all, don't call it work. Just call it what you do. I have just as much fun and passion sitting with a group of clients over a dinner as I do with family or friends. I'm not schmoozing clients. That's unhealthy thinking, and it's living to get, not to give. And you know how I feel about that.

Find something you love doing, and you'll never work again.

If you come from a giving place, the people you work with become your friends. So that's another aspect of it. This doesn't mean you won't have times in your life when you might be neglecting your friends or family. This also doesn't mean you won't miss out on a business opportunity because you committed to being at your daughter's soccer tournament.

You can't get to everything, especially if you have a rich life. I have an abundance of riches, from friends to family to business endeavors and activities that excite me. It's nothing to complain about.

Some people translate this abundance into being overwhelmed. "I'm too busy to get to everything," they say. Don't expect to. I never use the word "overwhelmed," and I never complain about being too busy. I highly recommend getting rid of those labels. They are transformational words that impact your mindset in a negative way.

Never underestimate the power of language and the influence of words and labels on yourself. Replace them with thoughts and expressions that speak to your passion. Say, "I live a big life. I'm in demand. I live a full life, and I use my time as best I can."

MANAGING ENERGY

Now we come back to the idea of managing energy instead of time. Do you think it gives you energy to label something as work? A lot of people use the word "work" as something they have to get over. They've done their work, and now they have to recover from it. They've put the category of "work" into a negative box.

Think about when you are playing your favorite sport. Are you complaining to yourself about how hard it is to improve your golf swing or your tennis serve? Are you grousing about how hard it is to train for a marathon? No. You have merged difficulty and joy. Why not do that with work? Don't complain about how hard it is. What makes it fun is the challenge, the difficulty, just like your sport. It doesn't "take" all your energy. You deliberately, intentionally use all your energy for your purpose.

I believe when you're excited about what you're doing, no matter how hard it is, the achievement gives you energy. When you view it as part of living a full life rather than paying some dues on one end so you can enjoy life on the other end, you won't dread it, and you won't need to recover.

For example, I love going to Europe. For years, I've mostly been unavailable for business in the month of June because for me, part of living a full life is making sure I get to do everything that gives me joy, and that includes vacationing. Even though my focus is not on business, I still check my email every day while traveling. Why? Because I love my businesses. I don't want to neglect them so I can "recover." I don't beat myself up when I work hard or call myself a workaholic. I'm just allocating attention to what I love, even when I'm in vacation mode.

I'm not doing it because I have to. I'm doing it because I *want* to. It's fun for me. And if I didn't pay attention to that, what else would I be doing? I mean, I can only eat so much pasta and drink so much wine in Italy. I can only see so many Roman statues.

Most people go on vacation and dread the day they have to go back to work. You should always have time and ways to recharge yourself, but why erase its positive effect by dreading when it ends? This is the trap of labeling something separate as "play." If it's to "get over" work, then it isn't a life-work balance; it's a constant trade-off of negative and positive.

I'm professing not to beat yourself up because you don't have this "balance." A great life can be a roller coaster ride, and that's a lot more fun than a wagon train.

And a few words about workaholics. To me, that's just a person who has lost track of their core values or hasn't even created them. They're getting all their significance from "work" and financial achievement. I've been there. Real balance in life happens when you live honestly, in service to your core values, as best you can, every day.

If you find you can't do this, take a hard look at the life you've designed for yourself. That's what needs to be fixed.

POWERFUL QUESTIONS:

- Do I put work in a separate negative category from play?

- Does my work contribute to my passion?

- How can I blur all my life's activities together as one joyful, challenging experience?

9

LIFE BY DESIGN

THIS PRINCIPLE IS BASED ON ONE SIMPLE FACT: IF YOU DON'T actively, specifically design your own life, someone else will do it for you. That may be your boss, your teachers, the government, or even your parents. Take a look around you and see how many people are living a life they seem to have designed. I'll bet it's very few.

As always, it comes down to asking the right questions, this time of yourself. The first question is, "What if I could retire right now?" I have a few thoughts on the concept of retirement, but let's use that word to mean you aren't required to work anymore to maintain your lifestyle. In other words, there is no financial need for a job.

LIFE BY DESIGN EXERCISE

I recommend doing the following exercise. Take a sheet of paper, and draw a line down the middle. Then, on the left side of the page, list everything you enjoy doing or want to be doing with your time. That can be work or play, using our new mindset about those. Then, on the right side, list the things you don't enjoy doing—the things you don't ever want or have to do.

By the way, I don't care if you work for the phone company or in food service or you're a CEO. Anybody in this world, in my opinion, can do this exercise. It's about getting clear on what you love to do and what you don't so you can begin to design your ideal life and future.

On the left side, think hard about what you want to spend more time doing. Populate that side with all the things that give you juice, that are purposeful and fulfilling to you. And be fanciful about it; don't impose limits on what's possible. Think of it as a game, an ideal of how you would like to spend your time while you're here on planet Earth.

Maybe you want to live in Europe every summer with your kids. Maybe you want to open a soup kitchen in your hometown. Maybe you want to play golf, tennis, or soccer three times a week. Or five.

Don't just do single events. Remember, you are taking the first step to designing the life you want. So what do your days involve? What will you do every month or every year? Who will you spend time with? Where will you live? What will you learn? What will you be attempting to achieve not for the money but simply for the gratification?

Now, turn to the other side of the sheet and start detailing all the things that steal your joy, where fun goes to die. Things that are just boring to you, that you feel are a waste of time, that are agonizing. Also, list the things you aren't good at doing. These may be things you are currently doing as part of your job or your personal life. They could be in your daily life, or they could just be things you never want to have to do.

Please don't think I'm implying you will be able to eliminate everything you don't like doing in your life. You may hate personal grooming, but there will be consequences to giving that up, and it will most likely diminish the quality of your life. Same with taking out the trash or going to the doctor or dentist for regular checkups. No life is an endless amusement park.

As an aside, I am constantly wondering why the hell people want to do things they're not good at. It puzzles me because I know that fulfillment comes from working with your strengths. I've learned that a lot of joy comes from excelling. So that's my bias. More on that later in the book.

This exercise is a critical step in creating a life by design. Get very clear about where you want to spend most of your time and where you don't. Bear in mind this exercise maps out what you will be changing over a period of time because it won't happen overnight. In addition, there are other elements to effectively design a life you want to live, like setting goals, which we'll discuss later in the chapter.

This exercise is meant to become a life habit. It should be something you reexamine on an ongoing basis, especially when moving from one phase of your life to another. For example, you may have a very specific design for your life until your kids finish college. After that, there is likely to be a major shift.

With this exercise, you are beginning the process of eliminating the things you don't want to do and increasing the ones that you do. It starts with a clear awareness of those things, just as building a house starts with an architectural plan. Your goal will then be to add and delete items over the next year or two to align with your design.

Look at your two lists. What if you slowly eliminated all the things on the right side and only did things on the left side? Wouldn't that be satisfying? And don't you have the power to start that right now? Why not? What's stopping you? Answer that question for each of the items on both sides, and you're halfway there.

THE PROBLEM WITH "RETIREMENT"

I think the word "retirement" is a horrible term. As always, transformational words matter. That word puts head trips and limiting beliefs on you. Society has laid it out for you to work all your life, doing what you have to do, until you have financial freedom. Most people don't ever achieve that because they don't save enough or Social Security doesn't pay anywhere near enough to lead a life by design. So they burn up their most energetic years doing what they don't like just so they can stop doing it.

It's time to rewrite this whole crazy script. I'm sixty-two now, and people ask me, "When are you going to retire?" My response is, "Why would I quit doing the things I love to do?"

That's my response because I've designed my life deliberately over a period of years, to a point where I'm the happiest I've ever been. And the reason is I no longer do the things I don't want to do. I don't go places I don't want to go, and I don't deal with people I don't want to deal with. Now, maybe financial freedom gives you some of those options. But it's not just about having money. It's about you guiding the direction and making a series of decisions that make life better, step by step, so you're enjoying the journey, not just the destination.

If you have a life of your own design, why would you ever "retire" from it? And by the way, I'm hoping you don't think I mean the end goal is sitting in an easy chair and watching the grass grow. People only feel the need to do that when they hate what they do every day for money. I still do really difficult things. I challenge myself all the time to get better. And I always will.

If you don't design your life, someone else will do it for you.

Remember what I said in the previous chapter about merging difficulty and joy? That's what I'm talking about here. There should be things in the left column that will take every bit of your energy and effort, but accomplishing them will give you joy. I'm still involved in starting businesses, exercising, and learning, but my daily and yearly activities are all my intentional design. I want a big life, right to the end.

There are tons of studies showing how short the average lifespan is after someone retires. I think that speaks directly to people having lived a life not by their own design, and then their retirement has no design either. I've met retired people who are now Uber drivers because they were bored to death with retirement.

They don't need the money, but they need to feel they're accomplishing something or interacting with people. They discovered their original "design" for retirement was a personal hell.

I'm well aware you can't eliminate everything in the right column with the wave of a wand. The process is to systematically reduce those things. Make them more interesting, or give them a purpose. Or find a way to eliminate them. If you could eliminate half of them, wouldn't your life be better? Two years from now, if you're down to doing 20 percent of those things, you probably won't care that a remaining one-fifth of your time is annoying, unpleasant, or tedious. You'll have time and space for the things that bring you joy.

Now, some people can't think of many things to put in the left column. They are so consumed with what they "have" to do that they don't even have a clear sense of what would give them joy, except for stopping what they're doing. It's just as important to become aware of what would bring you satisfaction, challenge you in a fulfilling way, and make it exciting to wake up and "get to" every day. If that column is thin, then you've got some work to do envisioning a better future.

YOU CAN CHOOSE

These two lists will be different for every human being. But I see misery and disappointment in so many people's lives because they didn't create an awareness about the choices they made. They let someone else design their rat race for them. Then, they just climbed onto the wheel and bitched about it for forty years, all the while believing they had no choice.

The first step is always awareness. By doing this exercise, it brings into sharp relief what's wrong with your life design and how to fix it.

Also, people make the mistake of thinking they have to do everything themselves. The activities in the right column have to get done, but could they be done by *somebody else*?

How much would you pay to *not* have to do those things? There's a powerful question. I can assure you if you deplete your energy doing things you don't want to do, you'll have very little juice left to do the things you want to do. What if you could make more than enough money to pay someone to do the things you don't want to do, and you could have the time back? What I've found is when you recapture that energy and apply it to the things you are passionate about, the money will always come. That is the essence of why life by design works.

I'm living proof of it, and so are the many people I've coached over the years. I have been on this path, refining it for close to thirty years. Going back to the concept of studies on aging and happiness, I believe many people in this country will say their sixties were the happiest decade of their lives. Why is that?

I think it's because they've finally created a balance between the money they have and the money they need, sometimes because they need less and other times because they've invested well. And they're able to stop doing the things they don't like to do. They also don't care nearly as much about what other people think they should be doing with their time.

So my question for you is, why wait until you're sixty-five to feel that way? Notice I didn't say people were happiest in their seventies because that's when health problems often set in or one spouse passes away. Why live your entire life aiming for one good decade? Sounds misguided to me.

Anyone can get on the path of what I call "retired in your mind" because it's not really about retiring; it's about having a great life in every decade—a life on your own terms.

LIFESTYLE REFINEMENT

I want to emphasize that designing your life is not about accumulating money. When I do financial freedom programs around the country, I always ask people, "Why do you want money? Why do you want a million dollars or fifty million dollars? Or a billion?" I ask this because very often they are only focused on a dollar amount where they believe they can relax and start to enjoy life. Once again, society has convinced us that having a big pile of money equates to happiness.

In reality, when you dig down, people want money not just for what they can buy but for the lifestyle they want to live. Money can give you that choice, to be sure. But it will only matter if you have refined what gives you joy.

As you spend more time doing what you love, you may find that you don't need half the money you thought you did. Suddenly you don't have to be a mega-millionaire, and you can eliminate more of the activities on the right side of the page. And you may find that you were actually wrong about some of these things you thought you'd love to do. They only sounded good to you because they seemed a lot better than the things you hated doing.

I've seen it happen where people say, "Oh, I want to go to Europe for two months every year." Then they find out after two weeks all they really want is a good cheeseburger and to be around people who speak English. How can you refine what gives you joy until you start doing it? And believe me, it is a process of refinement that will continue for your entire life. So start now.

SETTING GOALS

The other key part of life by design is setting goals for yourself. There is a separate chapter dedicated to goal-setting, but life by design is the main reason for doing it. Think of goals as a set of promises you make to yourself when you create a life plan. I have a series of promises in place in every area of my life. For me, it begins with emotional fitness, mental toughness, and all the emotions I want to live from. I am clear on what my goals are for each part of my life wheel.

You will also find that keeping those promises gives you energy. When I keep my promise of health and fitness to myself, I feel great, and I have way more energy. When I know I've given my wife the love and attention she deserves, I have the power to go out and act with love toward many other people. When I am on top of my finances, I sleep better and make better decisions. I have all the money I need to pursue fun, be generous, live comfortably, and share good times with people.

I didn't figure this out until my thirties, but at least I wasn't in my sixties. The sooner you start doing this, the better, but today is the best day to start.

What you do can either give you energy or deplete it. Since energy management is so important, I choose to start every day with a victory. Find that one thing you need to accomplish. It may be something difficult that takes two or three hours of focus, but after it's done, the whole day is wide open. That daunting thing is behind you as a win, and it will energize the rest of your day.

Maybe it's something you dread doing. Why drag it through your whole day, letting it diminish your joy because it's hanging over your head? Get it done right away, first thing, and release yourself. It's one of the magical tactics of successful people. They turn a difficult task into a win just by virtue of it being done.

A big part of living an empowered life is knowing you always have a choice. The worst thing in the world is telling yourself you have no choice. You always have a choice. I can't say that enough. If you don't believe that, then life becomes a series of obligations. But if you start shifting and choosing where you put your energy, everything turns around.

You don't have to transform your life radically in one day, and most likely that's not possible. But if you act every day with the intention of spending more time doing what you love and less of what doesn't bring you joy, the transformation will happen.

POWERFUL QUESTIONS:

- What would I be doing if I could retire right now?

- What is stopping me from eliminating each of the things I don't want to do?

- How much would I be willing to pay to stop doing those things?

- Do I start each day dealing with what is most important?

10

HUMOR AND A SMILE

The very core of my life philosophy is to approach every situation with humor and a smile. If you are familiar with the DiSC personality profile, I am a high "D," meaning I'm decisive and results-oriented. But "I" is my secondary trait, which means I'm enthusiastic and focused on relationships.

I mention this profile because it's important to understand yourself and what your tendencies are so you can then work your strengths while being aware of the negative aspects of those traits. "D" is my natural state, and I fall into it automatically; "I" is my adaptive state, which I move into more intentionally.

When I lead and work with teams, I work in my adaptive state. I suppress my "D" tendency because I don't think it's effective. I don't think it's a good character trait to be dominant and decisive all the time.

In business, it is necessary to be a "D" as far as making decisions quickly and sticking with those decisions. But I think my high "I" has created more of my success. I talk about the power to influence in the next chapter, and my belief has always been that if you're going to influence anybody, it's a lot easier to do it with honey than with vinegar.

Bringing in humor and a smile is about making things fun. My motto is, if it's not fun, I don't want to do it. Put another way, it's never too late to have a great childhood. This speaks directly to life by design. I approach business as a great game where you play hard, surround yourself with great teammates, and give it your all, but you never lose sight of the fun. Because it's all a game.

I think humor and a smile break people's armor down. It's a way to get around their shields and to get them to not take life so seriously. We don't do our best thinking and we're not our best selves when we're always serious. There are times to be serious, no doubt. But I think you can be laser-focused and serious and still do it with some levity.

You have to realize how powerful a smile is. A smile can change the world. It can soften a heart, lighten tension, invite cooperation, and so much more. And when you smile, the first thing that happens is *you* change, both psychologically and physiologically.

To illustrate this, I do an exercise in live seminars where I have the whole audience stand up, and I tell them to look up at the ceiling. Then I ask them to put the biggest, craziest smile they've ever had on their face and to just keep smiling. While they're smiling, I suggest they attempt to get depressed, to focus on the negative. They realize they can't do it. It's impossible. The positive emotion wins simply because of what we've done with our body.

By the way, it takes fewer muscles to smile than it does to frown. And how many people think they should only smile when they're happy? The fact is, they've got it backward. The science shows that if you want to be happy, you can start by smiling more. Why do we all smile for pictures? Because we want to look happy. And we do look happy in photos, with a smile we put on our face intentionally.

Your circumstances never define who you are unless you let them.

Many studies show that the hormones in your body actually change when you smile, elevating your mood. There was one study done back in the early nineties where they tested the clinical impact on a human being if they just smiled more. They took a group of clinically depressed patients and instructed them to look at themselves in the mirror and smile for ten minutes, three times a day, for no apparent reason. Just smile. The result for the patients was a radical reduction in their depression,

So if smiling works for clinically depressed people, imagine how it can work for you. Imagine if your reflex in a difficult or challenging situation or when meeting a difficult person was to make yourself smile? I adapted this practice a long time ago, and it's just plain magical. It elicits a positive response from the other person, even if they don't realize it. A smile is hard to resist.

Just think about how you react to a person who's smiling and looks happy as opposed to someone with a stern, grouchy frown. Why wouldn't you want to control someone's response to you in that same way?

Smiling is all part of living a better life. You start off with a smile, inviting others to do the same. And then you inject humor. I always make it a point to add humor, lightness, or levity to serious situations. It reminds people that in the end this is all a game, and we should be having fun.

PROPER USE OF HUMOR

Don't get me wrong. Humor can be misplaced. This is a life skill that requires timing and a keen sense about your audience. I tend to tease people. It's all in good fun because they know I love them. But it's never done in a way that makes them feel bad so I can get a laugh from the rest of the crowd. Humor done properly can gently show people that maybe their thinking is off, and the belief that they cling to might not be so solid. And because it's done with humor, it doesn't come off as an attack.

For example, let's say I am coaching a client, and he tells me about yelling at an employee who made a mistake, which caused the employee to get upset and quit. I might ask him, "Do you think maybe you didn't yell loud enough? Was that your mistake?"

I'll use a bit of sarcasm to get him to reflect on his behavior, and he'll likely start laughing and say, "Yeah, well, maybe I handled it wrong."

And now he's coachable.

I find humor and a smile effectively lowers the temperature in difficult situations, but it also lets people know you care about them and don't want them to be trapped in a negative frame of mind. I certainly don't want to feel that way ever.

Humor also gives people a chance to put things in perspective. It shifts the situation from adversarial to collaborative. As a result, success is much more likely, and you're more likely to build a lasting relationship rather than just make a sale or a deal.

Certainly, bad things will happen to all of us. Some of them are very serious. Tragic, even. But even at a funeral, I've heard people give eulogies, choking back tears, and then they tell a funny story about the deceased. They talk about one of their quirks, messy habits, or anything, and everyone laughs. It's a blessing, a gift of relief, and a burst of joy in a deeply sad circumstance.

I believe if you're going to live a happy life, if you're going to live a successful life, Humor and a Smile are essential. They are magical ingredients. You have to find a way to smile more and to laugh more at yourself and at life.

If you have the ability to add humor to a difficult, painful, or sad situation, you're putting it in perspective. That's what people lose when they get sad, discouraged, or depressed because something went poorly. They lose perspective, and they let it consume them.

Everything is just a small compartment of a bigger picture. When I'm coaching a dentist who's had a financial crisis, or maybe their best employee just resigned, I tell them, "Don't take it so seriously. It's just part of the game." So what if you came up snake eyes with that particular roll of the dice? It doesn't define who you are. Only *you* can define who you are. Your circumstances never define who you are unless you let them.

It comes right back to this: your attitude is a choice. Seeing the humor in a setback and being lighthearted about it is a choice. You don't have to be depressed, angry, or resentful. You don't have to blame God. It's a choice to do any of those things, and humor works way better.

When something terrible has happened, how often do we hear people say, "You know, I'll probably look back on this ten years from now and laugh"?

And to them I say, "Why wait?"

POWERFUL QUESTIONS:

- Do I actively smile throughout the day?

- Where can I bring humor into a challenging situation?

- Do I allow myself to see life as a game to be enjoyed, even when it is most challenging?

11

THE POWER
TO INFLUENCE

IF MY SUCCESS COULD BE SUMMED UP IN ONE SKILL, IT WOULD
be the power to influence. If you cannot influence people to your
way of thinking or to make a decision in your favor—to buy from
you, sell to you, work with you, or invest in you—your chance
of success is minuscule. In the previous chapter, we discussed
bringing humor and a smile to all your endeavors, which is
really just one step toward effectively influencing people. There
is much more to it.

Early in my coaching career, before Fortune Management, I
worked with a man named Pete Drubet, who had a franchise
with Anthony Robbins & Associates, which was one of the
programs Tony offered at the time. We coached any type of business, but it always boiled down to sales training. And that came
down to influence.

Influence is about reaching people on an emotional as well as an intellectual level. One of the companies we took on was a group of Wall Street stockbrokers. The first thing I taught them was not to hold the handset when they made cold calls. I recommended they get a headset and stand up and move around their cubicle space while they were talking. I explained how important it was to smile and laugh while they talked to potential clients and to project energy and enthusiasm. This one physical change had a radical impact on the effectiveness of their sales.

I've always approached business interactions this way so people could feel my energy and enthusiasm. Perhaps it was because of my nature, but I understood the effect it had on people. They can hear the smile in your voice over the phone, and something as simple as that can begin the process of influencing someone.

Let's go back to my formative years in business, when I developed this passion for influence.

THE EARLY DAYS

When I first started working with Anthony Robbins &Associates, I was at a crossroads in my life. I had just lost a million dollars in the restaurant business. To make it worse, I wasn't excited about any of the other businesses I was in.

I had started a tire store, but that was mostly because my dad was in the automotive business, so it seemed like a natural progression for me. I didn't really know anything else at twenty-two years old, but I didn't love it. It was just transactional.

Customers weren't excited about getting tires, and I wasn't really building relationships with them. So I kept looking for new businesses to create.

I went into real estate. A buddy and I created a real estate investment company. But at the end of the day, that business was transactional as hell too. There's not a lot of power or purpose to it unless you decide you're going to be an incredible realtor who helps people's dreams come true. But it wasn't like that for me. For me, it was about making money because that was where I was in my life.

That led me to create a public relations and marketing company for the casino industry. Why? Because I wanted to somehow combine work and play. I was a big gambler myself; I was always a risk taker and always in a hurry. In the beginning, my whole life was about shortcuts. The shortcut for me was getting my Nevada gaming license, and then I'd put these big junkets of high-rollers together, hosting golf tournaments and arranging all sorts of cool events.

At the same time, that business gave me the lifestyle I was looking for. I sat in the first ten rows of every major boxing match Mike Tyson ever fought at Caesar's Palace. The business opened doors to a very high-end lifestyle in terms of play. And along with that, I picked up a small limousine company because for me, it all worked in unison. I could take my big players into the casino and also have them driven around in my limos.

It seemed like a great lifestyle, but at the end of the day, it was not a purposeful enterprise because for me to make good money, other people had to lose it. The guests had to lose serious cash at the tables to justify the cost of these expensive junkets.

So what did I do? I created another business. This one was a restaurant. And of course, again, I was working toward combining business and lifestyle. I had a fantasy about the glamour of owning a successful restaurant. People would spend lots of money, and I'd walk around shaking hands, buying drinks, and all of that. I ignored the fact that with restaurants, there's an extremely high failure rate. I only saw the successful few, which to me seemed very appealing. I hadn't yet learned the concept of asymmetric risk, and I paid dearly for it.

I lost about a million dollars over a three-year period. I was a young man, barely in my thirties. I had a wife, two little babies, and lots of responsibilities. And a million dollars was worth a heck of a lot more at that time than a million dollars in the year 2021. It was devastating.

However, looking back, I'd say it was one of the greatest things that ever happened to me. At that point, I hadn't done a lot of personal development and hadn't learned emotional fitness at the level I know and teach today. But I did have enough of a positive attitude to ask the key question, "What's great about this?"

Of course, the immediate response was, "Nothing! Nothing's great about this at all. I've got to liquidate assets to stay afloat. I've got to recreate my whole life!" I wasn't happy about that. But if I hadn't run into those issues, I'd never be where I am today. It caused me to reassess what was really important in my life.

Naturally, it came down to the quality of the question I was asking. Before then, I was always asking, "What would make me more money?"

I realized the lifestyle I was so desperately trying to create was pointless. It was just indulgence and extravagance with winners and losers and no purpose to it.

I thought life was all about material gains. The insight I got from this crisis explained the error all of my decisions leading up to this time. Of all the five companies I had created, not one of them was purposeful, so they were bound to fail. It was a powerful realization.

Any time you buy and sell things and live on the margins in between, you're just a middleman. You're not creating anything, and you're probably not doing purposeful work. There are always exceptions to that statement. I think you could find your purpose by being a great real estate agent or car salesperson, but you have to do it with the right motives. Motives matter in life. They're critical.

The powerful lesson I learned was that making money is not a motive. I had people who depended on me, and I finally took the time to ask better questions: *What do I really love doing? What am I really good at? What am I really passionate about?*

I looked at myself and realized I was a gregarious person and a decent communicator. I had become a good salesperson and enjoyed that process. I loved building rapport with people.

So now, we circle back to discovering Tony Robbins' sales training division. I began to see how much I enjoyed influencing people and that it had become one of my strengths.

DISCOVERING MY PURPOSE

I got ahold of Pete and told him I wanted to develop my public speaking skills. I felt I could coach people to be better salespeople, and I was excited about it. We teamed up, and the more I conducted the training, the more passionate I became about it. I understood the power of influence and how it had worked for me, and I knew how to teach it.

Pete and I did sales seminars every weekend, and I honed my speaking skills. After a while, I realized the model wasn't sustainable because we couldn't have extended relationships with the attendees. Most of them were "one and done" customers. But it broadened my horizons to think about other similar things I could I do.

Over time, I discovered there was a drawback to our business. I was getting better and better at teaching influence, and people were learning powerful skillsets from us, but many of them were not high-integrity people. Some used good tools in ways that were not always good for others.

I concluded I had to combine my desire to teach influence with a higher purpose. The fact is, influence is agnostic. It's a skill that can be used to do good or to do harm. (Let's face it: Adolf Hitler was one of the greatest influencers of all time.) I had to marry my skill with a purpose where people would benefit. I had learned from the casino business that people losing so I could win didn't work for me.

This led me to Fortune Management, which offered long-term coaching programs for dentists.

FINDING FORTUNE

My initial reluctance to join Fortune Management came from my limiting beliefs. I said, "First of all, I don't know anything about dentistry. Second, I'm used to working with people who are out there going for it, like captains of industry, CEOs, and dynamic and motivated salespeople. I don't see dentists the same way."

Tony responded, "You don't understand. We're going to teach dentists everything you enjoy teaching. We'll teach them how to be leaders, how to market their services, how to grow a business. They don't know how to do any of that." That kind of interested me.

That same night I started to peel back the layers of the onion and realized that for the most part, dentists were a high-integrity group of professionals. And I loved Fortune's coaching business model because it was about building relationships and helping people turn their dreams into their realities.

That's what got me on the path to Fortune, and the rest is history. I had found passion and purpose, and I'm just as passionate today about sales training and the power to influence. I found real fulfillment because my skill to influence now had a purpose.

This power to influence is one of the master secrets of financial freedom and business success. Think about this. Nothing moves in this world until someone influences somebody else. Without influence, customers don't buy, investors don't invest, and the person you're in love with doesn't agree to marry you.

Think about your ability to influence as a parent. It can make the difference between your child becoming a CEO or the next US senator and ending up in a drug rehab center.

Here's what I've always told my children: I don't care what you decide to do for your living or your calling. I don't care if you decide to be a schoolteacher or a firefighter, write books, or create companies. The one essential thing is to do something purposeful.

Fulfillment comes when you combine influence with purpose.

Everything happens because someone influence somebody else. This is a skill you must develop and refine throughout your life. But if you look at my life, the lesson is also that you'd better have a set of beliefs about why influencing other people is good for them and good for you.

No matter what you do, no matter what company you represent, no matter what opinion or concept you're trying to influence, you'd better believe in your own product. You'd better believe in your own brand. You'd better believe that what you're selling is absolutely good for the people. Otherwise, you're just faking it. And that will catch up with you in the long run.

Also, realize that most of the time you can't achieve great success alone. You need a team. No matter your cause, no matter your mission, you have to enroll other people to take that journey with you. If you're the CEO of a company, your job is to influence every human being on your team to believe in the vision. If you're a sales manager, you need to train and motivate your sales force to propel the company's growth. If you're a dentist, you need everyone working in your practice to believe and communicate that your dentistry is a great value.

A key point I want to make is that passion, while essential, is not enough. You have to effectively communicate that passion. You need to refine your speaking ability, develop active listening skills, and become a master of asking powerful questions.

And most of all, you need to care. Just as important as being enthusiastic about your product and effectively communicating its value, you must make sure the other person knows you care about them and what's important to them. Without that, you're just manipulating them.

There may seem to be a fine line between the power to influence and the ability to manipulate people, but it's actually a wide gulf. Manipulators only care about themselves. An influencer offers something to benefit the other person, knowing if that person is effectively persuaded, they both come out ahead. There's a big difference.

The world moves through influence. This is a skill you will be refining your whole life. Become a student of influence, and your success will blossom. Simply put, there is no way you will find your fortune and have an incredible life if you don't commit to learning how to influence other human beings.

POWERFUL QUESTIONS:

- How effective am I at influencing people?

- What is my purpose in influencing people?

- How can I refine this skill?

12

BE THE BEST

When I say be the best, I don't mean try to be better than everybody else. Your aim is to be the best possible version of *you*. With everyone who works at Fortune and everyone we coach, we emphasize the importance of constant and never-ending improvement, or CANI. And that's how I approach my own life. I'll never be finished improving myself. There will always be more to learn. I will always need to adapt, grow, and change, with the goal of being the best me I can be.

And how could you expect to be static? You may be a great programmer, the best of the best, but if you don't learn a new coding language every five years, you'll be obsolete. Especially in the world we live in now, where change is becoming exponential, you have to be in a constant mode of self-improvement.

When I started doing live seminars with Fortune, I thought, *What's going to be my secret sauce? What is going to distinguish me as unique?* And the first thing that I decided was that when anybody came into one of my seminar rooms anywhere in the world, they'd get the full me—not just a repetition of information anyone could deliver. They might be able to get the information somewhere else, but my presentation skills would make it easier and faster to learn and adapt. The experience of *me* had to be unique. Even though my audience might be able to get similar information at a sales or personal development seminar, they would only be able to get Bernie Stoltz from Bernie Stoltz.

This led me to the self-improvement message I wanted to drive home. I wanted to teach people to create as much value as possible in every interaction—that clarified what being the best meant. The formula was simple: make a commitment that you will add more value through your chosen profession than anybody else in it. Because when you do that, the world beats a path to your door.

Any great entrepreneur succeeds because, in some way, they add massive value and then try to improve on that value day after day. They know the first step as a leader, entrepreneur, and innovator is to make sure they are the best they can be.

I realize that's a lofty goal, but that's the point. You want your impact and influence to be the most potent it can be. Most likely there will be someone better than you out there, but you strive every day to be the best possible version of *you*. When you do that, you will steadily rise to the top because I can assure you most people out there are settling for "good enough."

Very early on in my life, I began working for myself. I've never worked for anyone else since, perhaps because I was unemployable. But I always believed I would be financially successful. And that became real for me because I was able to crack the formula. I realized if I was going to have huge, lasting success, it had to be because I brought huge value. If I was going to constantly improve myself, I definitely wanted the people I worked with to benefit from that.

I do financial wealth programs all the time, and the attendees always ask how they can get to financial freedom and abundant wealth. I explain I'm going to give them several strategies and tactics to accomplish that, along with concepts about money they may have never heard. But I also say I can sum it up in one sentence: bring more value than anyone else in your profession.

Commit to adding more value than anyone else in your profession.

If you aim for that, how can you lose? This doesn't just apply to entrepreneurs; this applies to every job out there. If you are the best dental hygienist, carpenter, or financial manager, how could you ever lose your job? How could you not earn the top bonuses or be first in line for promotion?

The big mistake people make is they believe that if they simply put in the time, then they are entitled to the reward. Your boss doesn't measure how many hours you clocked in. What matters to them is the value you are bring to the company. If you say, "I've been here for five years. I deserve a promotion," then you misunderstand capitalism. You are confusing longevity with results.

Someone else will get that promotion. The odds are that it will be someone who brought greater value to the company than you did. I can guarantee you if that person is working every day to be the best they can be and you're just doing average work, then it's no contest.

THE FALSE BELIEF
OF ENTITLEMENT

I've never believed I was entitled to anything, and that is one of the things that has made me successful. I approached everything with the understanding that I was starting at zero. The rewards I gained would be commensurate with my contribution. That's a very exciting life. That's a very satisfying workday. I'm not waiting for the world to throw some luck my way or for some unearned opportunity or reward to land in my lap. Never allow yourself to get hung up on entitlement. That kind of thinking doesn't give you energy. It drains it.

If you start out with the belief that nobody owes you anything—which is the reality, by the way—then you know right out of the gate you need to create real value. Much of this book is about how to amplify that value, refine yourself so you are more influential, align your behavior with your goals, and develop life skills.

This concept of starting at zero is powerful. I like to use the analogy of the pro golfer. In professional golf, no matter how high you are ranked, you start every tournament at zero. The playing field is completely level at that first tee. Even if you are the top player in the country, if your score isn't high enough in the first two days, you don't get to play the rest of the tournament. And you make *nothing!* You are entitled to nothing.

Another mistake people make is they diminish the importance of what they do and use it as an excuse for not being the best at it. Okay, maybe it's not your dream job. But it's still important to be the best at it for two reasons. First, you will feel better about yourself, and you will feel like you're accomplishing something with your day simply because of a job well done. Second, and even more importantly, you will develop the life habit of being the best at whatever you do, so when you do figure out what you want to do with your life, you will have the skill and mindset to achieve at the highest level. So be the best window washer, valet, checkout clerk, or carpenter. This is about the journey, and you will look back and say, "I learned how to push myself. I learned how to make promises to myself and keep them, no matter what."

An important point to remember is that you won't win all the time, even if you are giving your best. Sometimes getting your butt kicked will be the result. But if you're smart, you will mine that experience for every bit of information and learn to become better. And you won't blame anyone or anything else for the failure.

THE PROBLEM WITH BLAME

Blame is a waste of energy. Blame deflects responsibility away from you, which means you've decided not to learn anything and not to improve. And hey, we all do it. It's a normal reaction. The trick is to only indulge that blame for a few minutes. Then, let it go forever, and focus on getting better. On your lifelong path to being the best, failure is full of valuable information. When you approach it this way, it's empowering, not discouraging. You are living your promise, not falling into victimhood.

If someone else in your chosen profession is currently making more than you, you need to take a deep look into what they're doing and what value they're creating that you aren't. Their current financial superiority shows you there are greater heights you can reach. Use it for motivation rather than feeling discouraged.

And this leads to another point. You can't just go by your own opinion of the value you are creating. The marketplace will tell you the truth. If you think you are getting better and better all the time but the results aren't showing up in more success, then you haven't figured out the correct value. If you haven't aligned your value with what the consumer wants, then you cease to exist in their mind.

Having worked with dentists for decades, I can give you a clear example from the dental industry. Many dentists believe the best way they can add value is by getting more and more clinical training. And that's certainly a good thing because you want to keep honing your treatment skills. However, they are surprised when their practice doesn't grow despite the number of clinical courses they have taken.

The reality is the dentist may not be the best at presenting their dentistry to a patient. Their influence skills may be lacking. Or their marketing skills. Or their leadership skills. They need their whole team to support the mission of case acceptance with their patients. Until the dentist turns their attention to the skills they need and focuses on being the best at those, the results won't be there.

The message is to listen to the marketplace. That's how you measure your value. And don't just be the best at what you like to do or what you think is fun or most interesting. Sometimes you have to refine skills that aren't fun for you. Being the Best isn't a joyride. You will struggle and bump into walls, and you will need to take a hard look at yourself. Even if you are great at something, you have to keep pushing yourself to stay great.

BONUSES AND BRINGING VALUE

A unique bonus system is part of what our Fortune coaches bring to clients, and we also utilize the same bonus format in our parent company. You must align your bonus system with results with the intent to create a win for everyone. In other words, if the customer wins and the business wins because of your contribution, then you should win. Notice the components there. Value has to be created for the customer, by you, and the business has to win as well. For example, if you make it a win for the customer by giving them a huge discount, the business doesn't win, does it?

Of course, the bonus plan needs to be designed that way too. If you are the best at your job and bring value from every direction, you will be rewarded. And that will be fulfilling because the reward will be based on what you truly deserve.

This same thinking applies to every relationship in your life. You want to bring value to your family, friendships, and fun activities. Why wouldn't you want to be the best spouse you could possibly be? The best parent? The best friend? You do that by bringing value.

But another key element, especially in relationships, is not to keep score. The key to living is giving. You give and add value without measuring if the other person is returning the same value. That's not why you're doing it. This is a higher level of being your best, where you don't measure to make sure you receive equal value. The reward is simply being the best person you can be in that relationship. Is it hard to do sometimes? Sure. But everything worth doing in life is hard.

Being the Best is also not an ego trip. When you are in constant improvement mode, that requires humility. You have to be willing to receive feedback, and that can be painful at times. But avoiding feedback is a guarantee you will miss areas of improvement, perhaps the most important ones. You will need to rein in your ego constantly. Being the Best doesn't mean *acting* like you're the best. It doesn't mean you are better than anyone else; you're just better than you were yesterday. The value you bring will determine if you are the best in other people's minds, and it's that value that matters.

Being the Best creates the stairway to your dreams. It won't be easy, and it won't always be fun, but you'll be in control of your destiny. If you are keenly aware you are starting from zero and the world owes you nothing, then you will summon the determination to work at being the best you can be.

It comes down to telling yourself this powerful truth: if it's got to be, it's up to me.

POWERFUL QUESTIONS:

- Am I constantly improving myself?

- What do I believe I'm entitled to?

- Where can I get feedback on my skills?

- What is the marketplace saying about my value?

13

WIN/WIN

THE WIN/WIN APPROACH IS VERY SIMPLE. ASK THIS POWERFUL question: does everyone involved in the transaction win? If not, don't do it.

I assess every situation, relationship, and company through that lens. It's magical. To me, it ties into karma and the laws of the universe. If everything you do is about making sure that everybody wins, you're not settling for a zero-sum game. I see the zero-sum game as the worst way to do business.

Why do so many people come from that mindset? Because they live in scarcity. They don't live in abundance. People who live in scarcity believe there's only so much to go around.

Some even see love that way, and that's terribly misguided. I know because I've proven the opposite to be true in my own life, and I see it with everyone who lives by win/win. Love is an infinite game. It's exponential. The more you love, the more love comes to you.

It's the same with business, and it ties into life by design as well. If you are approaching life as a zero-sum game, where someone has to lose for you to win big, then you are designing a life that will be unfulfilling in the end. You may get wealthy doing it, but you will have sacrificed the most important things for that gain.

When you see life as an infinite game (Simon Sinek wrote a terrific book with that title), the whole game changes. You come from a place of giving, and everything spirals upward. You create a gravitational pull of people who see life the same way as you and want to do business like you do. It becomes something very tangible, and it becomes your reputation.

Win/win creates a business relationship instead of a business transaction.

If the people in your world know you have an ironclad rule that everyone has to win or you're not playing, the word spreads, just as it eventually spreads if you leave a trail of devastation on your pathway to success. So there's a very practical long-term view to the win/win approach.

One of the keys to the win/win approach is not keeping score, particularly in relationships. If you are always truly leading with your giving hand, you don't need to measure if you got an equal return for it. You're not doing it for a return. The return could very well come from somewhere else or much later.

You're doing it because of the choice you've made: to live a life focused on giving, not getting.

In business, the win/win approach teaches you to compromise effectively by being honest with yourself about what you need from the transaction and what the other person might need. This approach creates a business relationship instead of a business transaction. If all you're doing is stacking transactions, then you are not playing an infinite game because once that transaction is over, you're back to zero. You start from scratch to find the next transaction.

I have built many business relationships over my lifetime, and honestly, I can't measure where I've won more or less in any of them. And best of all, I don't care because overall, I've had massive wins and tiny wins. Other people may have had massive wins because of my contribution, and that gives me joy because I don't come from scarcity. I treasure the relationships more than the reward, and somehow, that has led to more significant rewards.

But even if I made half the money I did, I would still be completely content with the outcome because those relationships are my true wealth, my true fortune.

IT'S NOT ABOUT MONEY

I have a good friend who created a business with a partner that lasted thirty years, and the two of them honestly couldn't say who took more money out of the company. They didn't care. They didn't calculate to the dollar who came out ahead. They both had abundant lives, and that was all that mattered. You may think that's foolish, but the fact is, after thirty years, they are still the best of friends. How many partnerships do you see end in acrimony and lawsuits, with the partners hating each other? It happens way too often. So maybe each of them leading with their giving hand wasn't so foolish after all. Maybe it was a big win/win, financially and personally.

The win/win approach leads directly back to life by design. If you are in a career that requires someone to lose in order for you to win, then you have to think hard about whether you want to stay on that path. You see these Wall Street traders make tens of millions of dollars a year, but often they promote a product where virtually everyone loses except for them and their company.

The net result is they have to spend insane amounts of money on their lifestyle. They need bigger homes, bigger yachts, private jets, and million-dollar wristwatches. They get depressed if they "only" make $90 million in a year when someone else on their team makes $100 million. Think about how absurd that is. But in my mind, this clearly demonstrates the failure of their win/lose approach.

This becomes a filter for me in designing my own life. To illustrate how vigilant I am about this, I only surround myself with people who also believe in win/win. I only do business with companies that believe in this approach. And I only support products and services from companies that share this philosophy. Otherwise, I'm forced to watch my back, or I'm apologizing to one of my clients for recommending a person, product, or company that lacked integrity. And I don't want to live that way.

Win/win is also the best way to get your team to rally together for the mission of your company. They can go out and sell because they know they are not only given permission to make sure the customer wins—they are *required* to. So they sell with greater confidence, and they know they aren't sacrificing their integrity just to make a buck.

This also means the company's design should be that everyone on the team wins when the company wins. They get bonuses and promotions based on the company winning. This creates full buy-in to the company mission. Conversely, in a zero-sum company, it's everyone for themselves. You know the size of your bonus means someone else got more or less—or none. It becomes cutthroat pretty fast in that environment.

I've also seen zero sum radically affect the longevity of a company. If you have a slash-and-burn or plump-and-dump strategy, then you'd better get out before it collapses in on itself. This is even more true in the world of transparency we live in. It's harder than ever to hide the fact you are always out for yourself or that your company is doing more harm than good. So why do it? You've only got one life. Why sacrifice decades by moving in the wrong direction?

This means you have to walk your talk. You don't sacrifice your integrity because a deal is too juicy to resist. Making a big score where someone else loses may be extremely hard to pass up, especially if you are struggling to achieve economic freedom. But trust me, you won't find your fortune that way. The money won't buy you happiness, and you can't buy back your integrity.

I can honestly say that in all of my businesses, if we figure we're in a win/lose scenario, then we're out. We won't allow our name to be put on the deal. Our brand has to mean something. So it's not just about doing win/win when it's easy; it's about *always* doing it. Every transaction, every relationship, every deal, every company.

Also, I understand there are no perfect human beings. We're all a mixed bag. We're all going to stumble, mess up, or go to the dark side every once in a while. But I'm giving you these principles so you know why certain victories feel hollow, why certain paths don't feel right, or why some seem to cost you more personally than what you gain financially.

The best we can hope for when we do slip and play a zero-sum game is to realize it no longer feels good. You don't feel like you beat someone. You just feel like you screwed up, and it's only a matter of time before the universe pays you back.

You can always course correct. You can wake up the next day and lead with your giving hand, and maybe someday even go back and undo or repair the loss you created. And I guarantee that will feel better than the win.

Once you start playing a win/win game, you'll want to do it more. It will feel better. It will always be enough. In fact, I want you to become addicted to it. For example, when you start exercising consistently and your body feels strong and healthy, you get to the point where if you miss a couple weeks of workouts, you start to feel bad. And then you figure out you need to get back to the gym to feel good again. Playing a win/win game will become the same way. Once you get hooked on it, the times you drift away from or violate it won't be satisfying.

Why not create the same addiction for yourself? Why not develop an uncontrollable need to lead with your giving hand and see the other person win too?

You also have to get comfortable with the possibility of walking away from deals. You may see the other person is determined to make you lose or tip the scales in their favor. They may be putting all the risk on you, making you pay beyond value, or trying to chisel you down on your price to the point where you don't profit anymore. So you walk away.

If you start settling for win/lose, with you as the loser, you'll get a reputation for that too. Win/win means you're included in the win. Equally important is walking away when you see a deal going down that will result in the other party feeling hurt or screwed over. You don't want to lose, but you don't want to create a loss for someone else either.

This leads to another point. When you measure the profit of a deal, don't think of it just in terms of money. The profit should also be measured by intangibles. Did you act with integrity? Can you be proud of this deal? Will the marketplace respect your business for the way this was handled? Will the other party think they won too? Will this reflect positively on your brand in the long term? You may end up making less of a monetary profit, but if the answer to each of these questions is yes, then you profited with integrity. That's the win you want!

Also, in situations when it's about a relationship, not about money, people fall into the trap of measuring winning by being right. It becomes paramount that the other person acknowledges they are wrong and you are right. How often does it happen that the other person admits they were wrong?

Approximately never, right? Part of winning is losing your attachment to being right. You have to decide what's more important: do you want to be right, or do you want the best result for everyone? Do you want to be right, or do you want to be effective? Do you want to be right, or do you want to be in a lasting relationship?

REINING IN THE EGO

Being right indicates your ego is in charge. And that almost never results in a win/win. As you grow as a person and cultivate a win/win mindset, you will find the more you put your ego aside, the easier it will be to find that wonderful middle ground. You will find as you evolve that the ego is the enemy. It makes you reactive, and it is also the driving force behind a win/lose mindset. At its worst, the ego decides it's more important for the other person to lose than for you to win. That's a failed life. That's why I say the ego can be the enemy.

Let me give you a paradigm to follow using a company I helped set up. The company, OraCare, had created an oral rinse that vastly accelerated the healing process for any procedure involving the patient's gums. (They later discovered it also killed COVID-19 in twenty seconds, but that's another story!)

I said to the partners, "Let's make sure this is a class three company at the outset." By that I meant it had to meet three criteria. First, it had to be good for the customer (in this case, that was the patient). Second, it had to benefit the industry (in this case, that was dentistry). And third, it had to contribute to the greater good, and we knew this product would help people be healthier in general. OraCare checked all three of those boxes, and now it is a phenomenally successful business with plenty of long-term potential.

If you can create a class three business where the customer wins, the industry wins, and it contributes to the greater good, then it's the ultimate win/win business. The company I've been CEO of for twenty-six years is a class three company. Fortune clients run their businesses more successfully and the dental industry is better off because we make it possible for everyone to evolve and succeed. As a result, more people are taking care of their teeth and are therefore healthier. This is why our coaches can get up every day fired up and raring to go. Because everybody wins.

Finally, I can honestly say I approach everything in my life believing there can *always* be a win/win. It just comes down to finding it. Am I addicted to that? You bet. I wish every person, every business, and even every country approached things this way. But it starts with you.

POWERFUL QUESTIONS:

- How committed am I to a win/win approach?

- How attached am I to being right?

- Who in my life sees the world as a zero-sum game?

- How can I make good on a win/lose that I created?

14

EMBRACE TECHNOLOGY

ONE OF MY SUCCESS SECRETS IS THAT I HAVE ALWAYS INVESTED in the best technology. That also means I've put it to use. At its best, technology makes us work faster, more efficiently, and more effectively.

Nothing frustrates me more than when people fail to take advantage of advances in technology. Often they use the excuse that it's too hard to learn. Sometimes you have to slow down to speed up. The most successful dentists I know are constantly adopting new technology so they can treat their patients with greater accuracy, do it more quickly and comfortably, and give a better result, often at a lower cost.

However, this doesn't happen because they buy the technology. It happens because they learn how to use it. Sometimes they have to change their workflow or get more training for themselves or their team members. So they do it. Why? Because they want to be the best at what they do. And I can tell you with absolute certainty that being the best will require you to Embrace Technology.

THE BENEFITS OF TECHNOLOGY

When used properly, technology gives you time back. Time is the most precious commodity in your life.

Technology gives you freedom. You can design a life where you work the hours you want with whomever you want.

Technology gives you exponential growth. If you have to do everything yourself, bake every loaf of bread, make every sale, you'll wear out fast.

How powerful is it that I can access any information I want about my business, or any records, dashboards, or communications, from any device, anywhere in the world? That makes my life significantly better. I work comfortably and seamlessly from two different homes now.

Technology also saves lives.

Fighter pilots used to be trained in actual planes. These multi-million-dollar jets would occasionally crash, destroying the jet and often costing the pilot his life. Now every pilot who flies any plane is trained on a simulator, whether it's a Piper

Cub or a space module. Nothing crashes, and nobody dies. Why? Because of technology, applied. And the pilots are better trained too. There are probably millions of examples of technology saving lives at this point in time, from airbags to cancer treatments and everything in between.

We are all facing an ever-accelerating level of technology in every aspect of life. Robotics, nanotechnology, biotech, genetics, 3D printing, quantum computers, and blockchain. It's dizzying, which means you have to keep up. And when you do keep up, it makes it a lot easier to create a business where everyone wins.

Now, I know you can become a slave to technology, but only if you let that happen. If you're crawling Facebook or Instagram for hours at a time, you are letting Mark Zuckerberg design your life. Which he is happy to do.

Run the technology. Don't let it run you!

The key is to run the technology, not let the technology run you. If you get trapped bingeing a Netflix series because they instantly start the next episode, then streaming technology is running you.

When we conceived Fortune Management, we decided to make the company virtual early on. We seized the opportunity for our people to connect without bringing them into an office. This created a company that could operate in any city in the country and give face-to-face service to clients at the same time, all while tapping into all the resources of the parent company.

When the pandemic hit in March of 2020, we didn't have to make a single change to our infrastructure. The only adjustments we had to make were moving our in-person seminars to Zoom technology and refining our messaging to help our clients get through this crisis and come out the other side with their business intact.

My warning to you about technology is this: don't adopt learned helplessness. As I said, some people use the excuse that some new app or new tech is just too hard to learn. They'll even say the old way was much better. But when I press them, they can't give a single example of where that was true. They don't say, "I'd much rather use a paper map. It's better." You know why? Because it's just not true. Google Maps not only tells you exactly how to get to your destination the fastest way, based on up-to-the minute information, but it also shows you a picture of the place you're heading to.

Do you think it was better when all medical records were paper, stashed in mountains of files in rows of file cabinets? Or is it better that your doctor can look up every procedure, medication, and appointment you've ever had at the touch of a key? Which one is more likely to keep you alive longer?

Right now, most technology has been designed so a fifth grader can use it. Are you really going to admit you aren't smarter than a fifth grader? Once again, it comes down to choice. Not adopting new technology is a choice. Refusing to learn new things is a choice. And all choices have consequences.

In our fast-moving, ever-changing business economy, those consequences may mean you become obsolete due to some seventeen-year-old who designed a better product than you in their basement. It may mean you're not staying in contact with your friends because they live too far away to get together, and you don't want to learn to use FaceTime.

It may mean you're working twice as hard as you need to.

Choices have consequences. Why not make those positive consequences of greater freedom, more time, and exponential success? It's up to you.

POWERFUL QUESTIONS:

- What technology am I afraid to adopt?

- Where have I behaved with learned helplessness?

- What technology could I adopt that would make my work better for me and my customers?

15

ABUNDANCE

I AM CONVINCED THAT THE MOST CRITICAL CHOICE A PERSON will make in their life is whether they believe in abundance or scarcity. That world view will govern their future more than anything else. If you believe there isn't enough money or opportunity or love to go around, your life will be completely different than if you believe there is more than enough to go around.

Having an abundance mindset has impacted everything in my life. And looking back, I see where it came from. As I have shared, I grew up in San Francisco with my young parents, and we lived with my great-grandparents in a big, two-story house. They had a vast garden where they grew everything imaginable and a cellar where they made cheeses, salamis, and also wine and grappa.

On the first floor of the house was this enormous kitchen, almost commercial size, and my great-grandmother, Nonni, was always cooking. In the dining area (not the formal one, which was upstairs with the formal living room, where no one spent any time because all the furniture was covered with plastic), there was a long table that seated at least twenty people.

One day I asked her, "Nonni, why do we have such a big table?" Her answer was simple and profound: "So there's always room for one more."

That's an abundance mindset in its simplest form. They were not wealthy people. My great-grandfather was a garbageman. But they always made room for anyone who showed up, and I can remember countless meals with crowds of people eating and talking and socializing. Maybe this was unique to Italian households at the time, but it infused in me this deep belief there was always enough to share.

Later in life, I realized the power of that belief. I also realized many people don't come from a place of abundance. Most people, I've observed, come from scarcity. And that affects almost every decision they make. Here is the most remarkable thing about mindset choice: whichever one you choose to believe, you will be right. Because you will create a life based on that mindset.

A scarcity mindset becomes the basis for a zero-sum approach. Somebody has to lose for you to win. A belief in abundance is the foundation for a win/win approach. You can live either way. But my years in life and in business have shown me that living in abundance creates a fulfilling life. Living in scarcity leads to resentment, manipulation, dishonesty, and, ultimately, misery.

I was blessed to learn this mindset early on from my wonderful Italian family. And there was a deeper dimension to the lesson. They operated from a place of abundance when they had very little. They were always struggling financially. Don't think for one second that you should wait until you are successful to live in abundance. The abundance belief comes first. If you have that when you start, even when you are struggling, you will build a life based on that foundation.

CHARITY AND GENEROSITY

There was a book written in 1930 called *The Richest Man in Babylon* by George S. Clason. It is a series of parables that are commonsense rules to financial freedom. One of the things that he talked about is the idea of being charitable even when you have very little. He explained if you don't learn to give ten dollars away when you only have a hundred, then you'll never give away $100,000 when you have a million.

This is an essential part of an abundance mindset. Many people believe they can't afford to be generous and charitable until they are wealthy. That comes from scarcity. When you learn to be charitable when it requires real sacrifice and you see the result of helping someone, you led with your giving hand. Then, you start to see accumulating money is not the point. It's what you do with it that matters.

This circles directly back to a life by design. Designing your life with an abundance approach when you start out with nothing creates an entirely different pathway. And it's a joyful one, I guarantee you.

The concept of charity is what I call a profound truth. Profound truths are things that were true a thousand years ago and are just as true today. There aren't many of those. "Do unto others as you would have done to you" is another one of them. Sounds like win/win, doesn't it? Charity coming back to you a hundredfold is another. Every major religion has some form of charity as a basic tenet, whether it's tithing, donating, or any form of giving.

I have found that my generosity and belief of leading with my giving hand have truly come back to me a hundredfold. I never do it because I'm going to get an exponential return. Because most often that return will not come from the place where I was giving and being generous. It will come completely out of left field, unexpected. This is what the belief in abundance creates.

If you come from an abundance mindset, you can weather anything.

It's also important to understand your abundant act may not yield a financial return. I may have helped someone out financially who was struggling, and years later I will get a letter from that person saying, "My daughter went to college because of you. You helped me when I was desperate, and I found my way back." When you get a letter like that, you don't need a check to go with it. Your heart will be full.

This principle requires that you give unconditionally. If you are constantly working from a precise measurement of getting an exact reward in kind for anything you give, you are migrating toward scarcity. Please don't misconstrue this to mean you should give all your money away and be foolish in your transactions. You get to include yourself in your abundance mindset. Remember, it's Okay to Do Well by Doing Good. When you believe everyone can win, you believe in a universe of abundance, and the universe will reward you. Sometimes it will be with money and sometimes with love, but always with fulfillment and the satisfaction of living a generous life.

With a scarcity mindset, you will always be putting conditions on everything. "I will only do this if I get that." Conversely, if you don't impose a condition of precise return before you act, you can lead with your giving hand. If you aim to add more value than anyone else in your profession, then you may very easily be giving more than you get in return. But remember, you're working to be the best, regardless of a precise conditional reward in the moment.

If someone comes to a lecture hoping for five good ideas, I want them to leave with ten. If someone invests with me hoping for a 20 percent return, I want to give them 100 percent. The abundance mindset frees you to give much more than necessary, expecting nothing in return, and you will become known as that type of person. But once again, that's not the reason you do it. You do it because you want to enjoy the liberation of abundance.

Scarcity is a cage you trap yourself in. You're constantly worried about coming out ahead. You're always focused on what you don't have, what there isn't enough of in your life. How many people live out their whole lives this way? Sadly, I would say the majority. It's no wonder people are miserable.

This circles back to our first principle, Gratitude.

How can you be worried about what you don't have when you're grateful for what you *do* have? If you're making five hundred dollars a week and giving fifty dollars away, you can choose to say, "Man, I could have bought something nice for myself with that money," or you can say, "How lucky am I to be able to help someone else who really needs that money?"

Abundance is an essential element to your emotional fitness. If you always come from abundance, you will have a lot less stress. You will weather anything because you believe abundance is right around the corner, either with new opportunity, a powerful lesson, or a great new relationship.

Scarcity, on the other hand, gives you permission to wallow in self-pity and blame the world for your problems. Not only is this a bad strategy for getting out of a deep hole, but it also makes you feel worse. Being grateful and believing in abundance will light the way for you and lighten your load.

Let's come back to the idea of being unconditional. When you live in abundance, you don't have to impose a condition on every transaction. I believe almost every parent loves their children unconditionally. But in work and relationships, most people have conditions. "I'll work this hard if I know I'll get a raise." "I'll be your friend as long as you don't need anything from me." When you love your child unconditionally, that means you don't expect them to be perfect. You allow them to be human and flawed, just like you. Why not make those allowances for everyone in your life? Why not start out unconditionally?

As Gandhi said most profoundly, "Be the change you want to see in the world." If you want an abundant world, an abundant life, it starts with you. You have to believe everything you need is inside you. It started at birth. You were given life, a body, a mind. And undoubtedly that life will come with challenges. The choices you make and what you choose to believe will determine the direction of your life.

From the day we arrived on this planet, we were seduced into thinking we needed certain things to be happy. But the bottom line is, we were born into abundance. All you need to have a great life is within you, determined by the choices you make, the things you believe, the actions you take. You may never get all you want in life. Nobody does. Sometimes you may not even have enough food. But you can always laugh, smile, and be kind to the people you meet. Love, the most abundant thing of all, is something you can always give. You were born with that.

If you don't make the effort to free yourself from the trap of a scarcity mindset, you'll never experience the power of abundance. Abundance is a blue ocean, an infinite game, just waiting for you to jump in. If you apply this single mindset to your life, I have no doubt you will find your fortune.

POWERFUL QUESTIONS:

- Is this action I'm about to take based on abundance or scarcity?

- If I am acting from scarcity, where did that belief come from?

- Am I willing to try an abundance mindset?

16

APPEARANCE MATTERS

THE PRINCIPLE OF APPEARANCE MATTERING COMES DOWN to this: whatever your profession, look professional. This doesn't mean you need to wear Zenga suits and a Rolex watch or Fendi dresses and Jimmy Choo shoes. It means you have to decide what's appropriate so your clients see you in the best light and have confidence in your capability. Part of this is created by how you dress and how well you are groomed.

Human beings are wired to make judgments about people based on their appearance. Many times it isn't accurate, but that doesn't stop us from doing it. This principle means you accept that people have biases. You won't be able to change that, so if you want to be successful, why make this harder on yourself? This is one element of the Power of Influence that you can't ignore.

This even applies to your physical fitness. In most professions, people are judged if they are overweight. Right or wrong, people believe it's a self-discipline issue, and you don't want to project that.

Again, this doesn't mean you need expensive clothes or to be built like a gymnast. You need to gauge what will have the ideal impact on your audience or your customers. If I'm in front of 5,000 people, you can bet I'm wearing a great-looking suit and shined shoes, and I have a fresh haircut. But if I'm in a meeting with dental clients in Oahu, I'm wearing a Hawaiian shirt and casual trousers because that works for them.

MIRRORING AND MATCHING

Taking care of your appearance projects that you take pride in yourself. Please understand how important this is. People respond to all sorts of subconscious cues about you, and it also shows you respect their time and their tribe. If I walk into a meeting of potential investors who just flew in from New York and they're in the meeting room wearing suits and ties but I'm dressed like I just walked off the golf course, I send the message that I'm a man of leisure. Will they be willing to back me with millions of their dollars? Maybe. But why would I take that chance?

This even comes down to the car you drive. If you are taking clients anywhere or they see the car you drive up in, they want to see that you can afford a decent ride commensurate with your level of success. You may not care about cars at all and just want the cheapest, simplest transportation, but 99 percent of the time, driving a Smart car doesn't make you look smart.

Your day-to-day Appearance Matters too. If you have employees, you want them to see you as a role model. If you are an employee, you want your boss or manager to see that you take your job seriously.

People may say, "Look at Steve Jobs. He wore a black t-shirt and jeans every day." My response is that when you're a billionaire, you can set the style. But in the meantime, think about mirroring and matching your audience and projecting appropriate professionalism.

For women, this can be an even bigger challenge. You want to be viewed as a professional. You don't want to distract anyone with attire that would be considered sexy. This is especially true if your client base or audience is women. If you wear a skin-tight dress with a high hemline, women will have a judgment about you. And it won't be positive, especially if the men in the audience are paying undue attention to you.

Conversely, you don't want to downplay your femininity to the point where you look like you don't care about your appearance or you're trying to make a statement. I've seen some women who deliberately make no effort to be well coifed or stylishly dressed to the point of frumpiness simply because they resent the fact that people judge on appearance. When you're a billionaire, you can make a statement. In the meantime, if your goal is to influence and go with the flow. Accept people's biases and leverage them in your favor.

Have you noticed that every male country singer wears a cowboy hat? Do you think they all have cattle and ride the range? Most of them don't even own a horse. But they make it easy on themselves by saying to the audience, "I'm one of you."

This is a perfect example of mirroring and matching. Whether it's me wearing a Hawaiian shirt in my Honolulu meetings or Tim McGraw in a Stetson, the audience is more comfortable.

Mastering appearance is an essential element in your power to influence. And it's an easy one. If you're aiming for a win/win, then look like a winner. It takes very little effort. You are greasing the rails to their acceptance of you, just like smiling does.

And speaking of smiling, as someone who has worked in the dental profession for three decades, I can assure you the condition of your teeth matters to people. If you use your smile to influence, you don't want people thinking, *Jeez, can this guy not afford to go to the dentist?*

Appearance is an essential part of influence.

It takes emotional fitness to take care of your body and your physical appearance. That's where the judgment comes in with people. If they think you're afraid to go to the dentist or too undisciplined to be well groomed, it lowers their trust in you. You are making it an uphill battle to influence them.

Dentistry is a good example of this. Let's say a dentist pulls into the parking lot with a twenty-year-old Mazda that's badly in need of a paint job, wears hospital scrubs, and has misaligned teeth that lean more toward yellow than white. How easy do you think it will be for that dentist to get patients to do an expensive cosmetic makeover?

Conversely, imagine the dentist has a nice new car, like a Lexus or Cadillac, wears a nice white shirt and a well-designed lab coat with the dentist's name and the practice's logo, and has immaculate, straight, white teeth. How much easier will it be for a patient to trust that dentist's recommendation?

As always, it's about striking a balance. You don't want to wear a $50,000 diamond pinkie ring if you're selling cars. The average customer will think you're too slick and that they won't get a good deal. If you show up to your speaking event in a Bentley, you'd better be teaching your audience how to become millionaires, not how to make their Pinterest accounts more active.

A lot of the time you can't figure this out on your own. That's not a good excuse. There are people who do this for a living. You can hire a styling consultant who will help you design your wardrobe based on your profession and recommend an appropriate hairstyle. It's an investment that will pay for itself tenfold, if not a hundredfold.

You will also discover that when you look good and your appearance makes a positive impact, you *feel* good. Some people even have lucky clothes. I personally have lucky underwear. No one knows it, but when I have it on, I'm unstoppable!

You will also have to adapt your style over time. Don't think this is a one-time adjustment. Hairstyles change, and fashion shifts. It may be important to always have a trendy look for your career, or it may be more appropriate to look classically professional. But don't think your style is set for the next thirty years. That's highly unlikely.

POWERFUL QUESTIONS:

- What do my appearance and attire project?

- Am I mirroring and matching my audience?

- What is considered appropriately impressive for my profession or in particular situations?

17

DOING YOUR HOMEWORK

Let me start with a quote from the Roman philosopher Seneca: "Luck is what happens when preparation meets opportunity."

Too many people wait to get lucky so their lives will fall into place and their dreams will come true. This principle of doing your homework turns that idea on its head. Most often, it's preparedness that creates the luck because when an opportunity shows up, you recognize it and have the skill to seize it.

That's a much better plan than hoping to get lucky. Wishing for luck to come your way is saying you are not in charge of your life. Being prepared for when opportunity appears is a life by design. So here we are again, asking a crucial question: "What skills will I need to achieve my goals?"

If you reverse the process and only start your learning after the opportunity presents itself, why would you expect to succeed? That certainly limits the odds, in my experience. This also harkens back to always Being the Best, no matter what job you're doing. Operating from a mindset that you will always do your best work, even though it may not be fulfilling or exciting, is preparation. You do your homework so when the opportunity shows up, you're ready.

Every single job I've had, whether it was washing windows at a gas station, running a limo business, or any other endeavor, prepared me for working with Fortune Management. When that opportunity came, I had already learned how to manage my finances, I had refined my speaking skills, and I had learned how to influence people. I had learned to work hard at whatever I was doing so that when I got to my dream career, which my abundance mindset assured me was coming, I was ready.

If I had not done all that preparation, it wouldn't matter if Tony Robbins's organization appealed to me. I wouldn't have had the skills to execute at the highest level. I may not even have been offered the opportunity. Instead, as we developed Fortune, they invited me to become CEO. Was that just luck?

Opportunity also requires you to be in the right place at the right time, but you need to be able to recognize what the right place looks like. You have to put yourself in those environments. To know that it really is the right time, you have to be keenly aware of what the marketplace is interested in, and that means doing your homework.

HOMEWORK MEANS
PREPARATION

Doing your homework applies to developing your skills for the long-term achievement of your goals, but it also applies to your day-to-day meetings and activities. If you're about to have a meeting with your boss about a promotion, then you need to be prepared to show what you've done to deserve it. If you're raising money for your new business, you'd better have done all the research on the competition, laid out a full set of expenses and projections, and considered every challenge you might face. You also need to be damn good at presenting.

You wouldn't believe how many people come to me with a good idea for a business and want me to invest, but then I find they haven't done their homework. Sometimes they don't even know who else might already be doing the same thing. They haven't even researched their competition. It shocks me. Being a great salesperson doesn't mean you're just good on your feet. It means you know your product backward and forward. You understand what that specific customer needs and cares about, and you know the marketplace. This won't happen without doing your homework.

In a way, even your failures fall into the category of Doing Your Homework. Always mine your failures, asking the hard question: "Was I prepared enough?" Examining what went wrong, without ego, and learning from that is another step in doing your homework.

I'll give you a great historical example of when doing your homework made all the difference. Back in 1986, President Ronald

Reagan first met with Soviet President Gorbachev in Geneva to discuss nuclear disarmament. The implications of this meeting would be far-reaching. Reagan was a master communicator, based on a lifetime of training that began with acting and then serving as governor of California. So he was prepared on that level. When talks got heated and weren't progressing, he did was what called a "pattern interrupt," which is a negotiating technique. He stood up and said, "Gorby, let's take a walk."

The two men put on their heavy coats and walked outside in the bracing Swiss mountain air. And then things shifted. The conversation became friendlier. Reagan's negotiating skills, honed over decades, prepared him for this very critical situation. But he had also done his homework for this specific meeting. He knew from satellite photos that Russia's wheat crop had failed the previous harvest. This gave him something to negotiate. America had vast wheat surpluses. He knew what Gorbachev needed, and he had it. And thus the historic Strategic Arms Limitation Treaty was signed.

Successful people don't wait to get lucky to start preparing.

Great leaders don't wing it. They do their homework. Successful people prepare for the long and short term. Don't wait to get lucky. Prepare yourself diligently so when opportunity knocks, you're ready.

I will be the first to tell you I have had tons of opportunities. Maybe it's because I believe in abundance. But I've also missed some amazing opportunities in my life. Looking back, the question I ask myself is, "Was I ready?" And it always came down to a lack of preparedness.

How many people missed out on bitcoin because they didn't understand blockchain? I'll grant you, it's hard to wrap your head around it. But it's a perfect example. Were people who bought bitcoin in 2015 lucky? Or even 2020? Sure, but it's because they figured out what it was, how it worked, and how to buy it. I also know several people who've lost money on bitcoin, sometimes twice. Was that bad luck? I would say no. They were just reacting to something they heard rather than doing the difficult homework.

Even when it comes to relationships, you need to do your homework. Take something as simple as going on a first date. Find out if the person is allergic to shellfish before you suggest your favorite lobster place. And maybe learn their political views, too, so you don't put your foot in your mouth.

I've spent a good part of my life learning how to be a good spouse. That doesn't come naturally. It takes work. And why would you try to wing it as a parent? This may be the most important role of your life. There are tons of books and courses on how to parent wisely. Use those resources. Do your homework. Otherwise, you're in reactive mode, and you echo your own parents' words and behavior, or you let your emotions take over.

All of life is like this. Having a dream or a goal without doing the work is just a fantasy. You want to be an entrepreneur or do big real estate deals? How are you preparing for that? It's important to set your intention, but always know you've got plenty of work to do to get there.

I'll end with another Greek, Archilochus, who said, "We don't rise to the level of our expectations. We fall to the level of our training." doing your homework is your training.

If you believe in abundance, you will find that opportunities will always appear. You won't want to miss them. Be prepared. Do your homework. Then, when luck comes your way, you'll be ready.

POWERFUL QUESTIONS:

- What skills do I need to accomplish my goals?

- If I didn't succeed, how could I have been more prepared?

- Am I counting on being lucky to succeed?

18

CREATIVITY COUNTS

I DON'T CARE IF YOU'RE LEONARDO DA VINCI, LEONARDO DiCaprio, or Leo the barber. You need to tap into your own creativity.

I always tell people I'm not the most creative guy in the world, from an artistic standpoint. But I've spent my career taking something that was already there, whether it be a business, a concept, or a presentation, and finding a way to improve it. That's where I'm most creative.

Some people are massively creative. They come up with a lot of original thoughts, and they dream greatly. And I think that's fantastic. I think that's how humanity evolves. I think that's how new inventions come about. But I want you to understand you don't have to be the next Steve Jobs or Elon Musk. You don't have to have that degree of creativity to be massively successful.

The type of creativity you need is the ability to come up with solutions and find creative ways to solve problems. Some of the greatest companies were created by people who saw problems that didn't seem to have solutions, and they used their knowledge to solve those problems. Often, they didn't invent anything at all but just brought ideas in from other places. For example, 3M created the Post-it Note. But hundreds of types of glue had already been developed. They didn't invent notes or glue—they just stuck them together.

Most of the time, your business creativity results in seeing the world a different way, imagining something better, and coming up with new approaches. Bill Gates didn't invent the computer, but he believed there should be a way to put a computer on everyone's desk.

Often you can take something good and see a way to make it better. That's still being creative, and it's a skill you can refine.

My success has come from that mode of creativity. Whatever business I was involved in, I always asked myself, *How could I do this differently and make it better?* Even something as simple as adding a limousine business to my casino event business enhanced both of them by linking them together.

Often, I will hear a story and realize it could make a presentation of mine much more powerful, so I integrate it into my lectures and coaching. Creativity can appear in a series of small things that add up to big things. Or you can adapt things from one business model to another. Fortune Management began as an extension of Tony Robbins's teachings, but we refined and enhanced our programs to focus on solutions directly related to healthcare. We have continually built on those solutions, and we have pulled great ideas from many sources.

REINVENTING THE WHEEL

You often hear this expression spoken as a criticism: "Let's not reinvent the wheel." Why not reinvent the wheel? Creative people do it all the time. There are bicycle wheels that cost $7,000 a set, and everyone in the Tour de France wants them.

Most successful businesses are derived from existing business concepts. Steve Jobs reinvented the cell phone. He wasn't even in the mobile phone business, but he envisioned something better. He combined a phone with a computer and started a technological revolution.

He may have invented several little things along the way, but those were mostly components. His skill was to innovate what already existed. He didn't invent digital music storage. Sony did. But he made the iPod—he envisioned it as better.

He also used existing resources. This will be a critical aspect of your creativity. You have to constantly learn what resources are available to you. People do this with software all the time. They see a block of computer code that does one thing, and they realize it could have a whole different application. They don't invent a new computer language. They apply the existing code to their purposes. Look at companies like Uber. Without smartphone apps and GPS, they wouldn't exist. Most of the time, business creativity is about refining, adapting, or expanding something into a new arena.

And of course, technology is a huge part of it. This is why one of my principles is Embracing Technology. You need to know what advances are available to feed your creativity and help you solve problems in a new way.

The key to using creativity starts with giving yourself permission to dream greatly. If you have a goal, your mind begins to look for solutions. If you let yourself envision something, very often the elements start to present themselves. Don't get trapped in just thinking about what is. The magic happens when you think about what *can* be.

This starts the process of innovation, which always happens in your mind first. When someone tells you, "That's not possible," your response should always be, "Not yet." Have a vision that stretches you in fanciful ways.

LIMITING BELIEFS

A lot of my coaching work has involved coming up with creative ways to get people unstuck from their limiting beliefs. I know that for them to be successful, they need to have a vision they believe in, otherwise they'll never create a plan to get from point A to point B.

Most people's reflex is to come up with reasons something can't work. That's not innovation. That's not resourcefulness. That's victimizing yourself with a limiting belief.

Nothing stifles creativity like limiting beliefs. When I began working in practice management, I had a set of empowering beliefs. And one belief I still have today is that there is no business I can't grow or make intrinsically better through coaching, better strategies, and innovation, along with calculated risk-taking and resourcefulness.

I may suggest to a dentist, "Five years from now, you could have three practices, make four times the money you make now, and work two days less each week." And their response may be, "I can't imagine that." I will immediately respond, "That's the problem. You can't imagine it. It's time to start imagining that you can do it." And suddenly the gears start turning.

As I mentioned earlier, one of the principles Fortune has always espoused is the idea of constant and never-ending improvement, CANI. We don't just espouse it; we embrace it. And not just in business but in every aspect of our lives. We are always improving, and we will never stop improving.

Ray Kroc, the founder of McDonald's, said, "When you're green, you're growing, and when you're ripe, you rot. There's no in-between." Put another way, if you're not moving forward, you're moving backward. There's no standing still. Moving forward is what a vital life is about.

The parallel of this is the Japanese concept of *kaizen*. Most people don't realize that Japan's emergence as a manufacturing powerhouse actually came from an American named Edward Demmings. After World War II, the United States committed to helping Japan recover from the devastation of the war. We sent Demmings there to help them rebuild their factories.

Demmings had a concept called TQM, total quality management. He believed every product and every system could be improved upon over and over. More importantly, he believed that focusing on quality always cost less in the long run. This is a powerful concept: the pursuit of quality with a vision for the long term costs less. Sacrificing quality may yield quick, short-term results, but in the end it catches up with you.

And because of *kaizen*, Japan started making cars that were better than the ones coming out of Detroit, and doing it more affordably. Meanwhile, US automakers had started embracing the concept of "planned obsolescence" as a way of getting people to buy new cars every few years. By sacrificing quality, they made it easy for Toyota and Honda to come into the US market.

And then there were Sony, Mitsubishi, and all these other companies innovating and putting out well-made products. Prior to that, "made in Japan" meant cheap, low-quality junk. Everything changed because of one single principle. Japan imagined something better and figured out how to do it, knowing that investing time, energy, and money into better quality would pay off in the long run.

Lasting success is a constant learning process, and it's exciting because it inspires creativity. I can always make a lecture better with a new turn of phrase or perfect analogy. Or I could discover a new software or technology and introduce it to my clients. It's never-ending, and that's fun of it. There's always more to discover. You can always imagine a better future.

DREAM BIGGER

Most of us don't dare to dream big. We dream safe, and we fear failure. But everyone has an imagination. Why impose limits on it? Let's talk about one of the most creative geniuses of our time, Walt Disney. This is a man who imagined cartoon animation, a movie studio, Disneyland, Disney World, and Epcot Center.

There's an interesting story about the opening of Epcot. Walt unfortunately passed away the year before it opened. At the opening ceremony, one of the journalists asked Walt's brother Roy, who had taken over the business, "Don't you think it's kind of sad that Walt never got to see Epcot?"

And Roy's response was perfect. "You've got that wrong," he replied. "My brother *did* see it. And that's why you're seeing it today!"

Creativity starts by believing what you imagine is possible.

Walt always kept expanding his vision, seeing what could be. He never limited his imagination. Disney employees are still refining and improving their products every day. And you know what they call themselves? Imagineers.

Now, as a human being. here's where *kaizen* comes in. Once again, it's about reining in your ego. If you are humble enough to believe you can be better, then you will never be stalled by believing you have made it, that you can't improve. Remember the principle of Being the Best? That requires *kaizen*. And again, I don't need to be better than anyone else—just better than I was yesterday.

Success always comes down to your mindset and mastering your limiting beliefs. I'm an avid golfer, and I'm always trying to be the best I can be on the course. I know there are golf pros who are way better than I will ever be. But I can be a better player next time and find new ways to improve, often just by getting my head straight. Like most of life, golf is a head game.

It's been demonstrated statistically that if a golfer gets a birdie on one hole, they are much more likely to get another one in the same round of golf. Why? Because what they imagined as possible became real, so they believed it was possible again. This is the trick: to always believe what you're striving for is possible. Longtime golf champion Bobby Jones said, "The toughest course I ever played was the six-inch course between my ears." Ain't that the truth?

Kaizen can be applied to your lifestyle and your relationships, not just your work life. Your life by design means you always believe you can improve your lifestyle, not necessarily by buying more stuff but by increasing the quality of your daily life. You can creatively figure out how to spend more quality time with your kids. You can get creatively romantic with your significant other. If you want it and believe it's possible, then creativity, innovation, and resourcefulness kick in.

But something more is necessary. There are five key steps to success. They are:

1. Know your desired outcome. What are you aiming for? What's your vision?

2. Know your power. Believe in yourself and your passion.

3. Take massive action. Nothing changes until you do something. Make it something big.

4. Monitor results. You must see if you're going in the right direction and making progress.

5. Persist.

The fourth step is critical because you don't want to waste your energy and resourcefulness by moving in the wrong direction. You will most likely need to course correct. A lot of *kaizen* is exactly that. Change your approach. Pivot. Unlearn some things you thought were true. Listen to the marketplace. There's an adage that states, "You can chase the sunset with all your heart and soul, but you'll never get there if you're heading east."

People often fall short with the fifth step of persistence. They do the first four steps and get discouraged when the results aren't what they expected. But you can never give up. If I've seen one single common trait among all the successful people I know, it's that they can't be stopped. Failure doesn't stop them. They just change course. They learn and grow, and they get up and go again. They get more creative. They look for more resources.

How long should you give a child to learn how to walk? The question is ridiculous, isn't it? Because the answer is that you would never give up. And that child will never give up until they learn to walk, no matter how many times they wobble and fall. But as adults, we give up all the time. Why? We lose our belief in the power of persistence. We get discouraged by mistakes or embarrassed by failure, and we stop trying.

Except for successful people. Successful people just keep learning and trying to find a way, find an answer, and refine their vision, even though they know it will be hard. But remember, kids don't just learn to walk. They learn to run. They learn to dance.

Create, innovate, and be resourceful in the pursuit of your dreams. That's the great dance of life.

POWERFUL QUESTIONS:

- How am I limiting my vision of what's possible?

- In what ways am I creative?

- What do I need to learn? What resources do I need?

- Who can help me reach my dreams?

19

BELIEFS ABOUT PEOPLE

To be able to lead with your giving hand and seek a win/win in every situation, you have to have certain core beliefs about people. One profound truth I will remind you of throughout this book is that every belief we have either empowers us or holds us back. Whether that belief is 100 percent true doesn't matter. You can find evidence to support whatever negative or positive thing you decide to believe. What matters is the effect those beliefs have on you. In the chapter on abundance, I said that whichever you choose to believe—that the world is scarce or abundant—you will be right. Because you will create that world.

Each of us has beliefs about human beings. Often we are not even conscious of these beliefs, but they are reflected in our actions. But before I tell you my beliefs, let me be clear. I know we all have built-up prejudices based on what our parents taught us, our experiences, and how our peer group behaved. Those beliefs were formed without your consent or conscious effort. Some of them helped you in life, and some of them hurt you.

What I'm talking about now is taking conscious control of those beliefs so you can have a successful, fulfilling life. Again, it comes down to asking powerful questions. You need to dig into yourself and determine what you believe about people. And now that you know about life by design and win/win, you can ask if those beliefs support those principles or inhibit them.

People are essentially good if you give them half a chance.

I was lucky enough early on to realize that if I wanted fulfilling relationships and wanted to influence people effectively, I needed certain beliefs. The first belief I have held fast to is that people are essentially good if you give them half a chance. This belief in the essential goodness of people is foundational to how I approach leadership, friendship, and every interaction.

Am I right all the time? Of course not. People will disappoint you, and you will disappoint people. We're human. But if you let that warp your core belief and turn it into the belief that people are essentially bad, then you will be in defensive mode all the time. And you will be on the road to misery.

Remember, if you believe that about other people, it also means you believe that about yourself, and you let yourself off the hook for creating win/lose situations. If you get comfortable leaving a wake of destruction, you'll wonder why you have no love in your life and no real satisfaction.

THE TRUTH ABOUT
HUMAN RESPONSE

I believe you get what you give. It's the law of attraction, which I will dive deeper into in another chapter. I also believe people do the best they can with the resources available to them at that particular juncture in their lives. I believe everyone has resources, but I also know people sometimes put themselves into unresolvable states of mind, where they don't believe they have choices or options. I'll say it again: we always have choices. But I make allowances for people when I see them in that negative condition, knowing what causes it.

I also believe what I consider to be another profound truth, and this comes directly from *A Course in Miracles,* by Helen Schucman: every reaction you get from another human being is either a loving response or a cry for help.

This is an amazing prism through which you can look at your interactions with people. And I understand it's not always obvious—it may appear to be something else. Most people are good at a loving response, but often it is very subtle. How many siblings can never tell each other they love each other? Yet their actions show love throughout their lives. Most of us can feel love, but it takes work to express it, to let it flow easily and openly from us.

Don't assume a loving response will come naturally to you. You have to work at it, perhaps your whole life. But the better you get at it, the more satisfying your life will be.

I'll give you a lesson I learned years ago. Once I became successful, I became the person who always picked up the check. Maybe this came from my great-grandmother always wanting to feed everyone, but I paid for clients, employees, friends, everyone. Once I was with a friend of mine and, as I was reaching for the check, he stopped me and said, "No, Bernie, I got this one."

I rolled out one of my usual lines, like, "I got it. I had a good month," or "Nobody pays in my town but me," or something like that.

And he said, "Don't get me wrong. I appreciate your generosity. But sometimes you have to let other people do things for you. If you don't, you're depriving me of the chance to be generous."

This was a huge aha moment for me. I was good at giving love but not so skilled at receiving it. I realized it was important to receive generosity, compliments, and help from friends graciously, knowing I wanted to allow them the joy of giving. What a great lesson for me.

Identifying a loving response can be fairly easy. Where people get tripped up is with a cry for help. Cries for help are often disguised as something else. They often appear as an entirely different emotion. They will masquerade as indifference, resentment, or anger. A cry for help may come in the form of criticism, a complaint, or an accusation.

After someone's reaction, you may think, *This doesn't sound like a cry for help*. If that person is being mean to you, is angry with you, or even attacks you, it's hard to see that as a cry for help. You have to unmask the reaction. The only way you can do that is to believe people are essentially good and that there are only two possibilities for their behavior. Since it's obviously not a loving response, you have to make the choice to see it as a cry for help.

Unfortunately, human nature reacts in kind. When someone pushes us, we push back. When they attack us, we get defensive or even attack them back. This is your ego taking over. Now it's two people crying for help, masked as anger. And most often it amplifies itself in the wrong direction.

If you make the more evolved choice, the more difficult choice to release your ego, you can ask, "How do I see this as a cry for help?" You are then moving in the direction of a solution. You are responding with love rather than with another cry for help.

I'll take this to another level. Imagine if you saw violence as a cry for help. Think about how that would change what you believed about that person. How would you respond?

The truly great leaders in the world are capable of this. Mahatma Gandhi, Martin Luther King, and Nelson Mandela all believed that only love could conquer hate, and the most powerful choice was to be an instrument of peace. Nelson Mandela was imprisoned for twenty-seven years. He could have let his resentment build—justifiably, as he had done nothing wrong. He could have started a violent revolution upon his release. Instead, he reached out to his oppressors and asked how they could all work together to heal their country. That's the power of a loving response.

Ego leads us to react violently—to start wars, even. It also leads us to start personal wars in business, in our marriages, or against people with whom we disagree. The ego needs to be right. The ego separates us. Believing we need to respond to a cry for help with a loving response is founded on the belief that we are not separate, but rather, we are all connected as human beings. And that's a powerful place.

If you are reacting to anger with anger, hate with hate, and mistrust with mistrust, then you are doing just that: reacting. You are not choosing. You are surrendering your ability to choose your reaction to your ego. Why would you want to live that way? Do you believe you have no choice? This is a belief you might want to challenge.

I also believe every person is a mixed bag. No one is perfect. We all have moments of weakness, blind spots, biases, and deep wounds. Believing this allows me to hear the cry for help through the anger or accusation. I am flawed like everyone else. But now I can catch myself when I see I'm not coming back with a loving response and correct it—if not in the moment, then later.

Think about what a person has to believe about people to pursue win/lose outcomes. You have to believe you are on your own. You're the only person who matters, and you're against everyone else. This is the most extreme version of the scarcity belief. Even if such a horrible thing were true (based on my whole life, I know that it is not), why would you want to live that way?

I believe deeply, with every fiber of my being, that people are basically good. And I will always give them a chance. I will always lead with my giving hand. And I will do my damnedest to respond to every cry for help with a loving response. I hope you will too.

POWERFUL QUESTIONS:

- What do I believe about people?

- Which of those beliefs do I need to change to be successful?

- Which of those do I need to change to create win/win?

- Which of those do I need to change to attract and influence people?

- What do I need to believe about people to always offer a loving response to a cry for help?

20

BE A GREAT LEADER

One of my goals for you with this book is for you to become a leader. In fact, I want you to become a great leader. Being a great leader involves much of what we've already talked about. A great leader comes from a place of abundance. A great leader knows how to influence people. A great leader is creative and resourceful. A great leader never gives up. A great leader sees the best in people.

Let me elaborate on the last point. A truly great leader sees more in their people than they see in themselves and encourages them to become greater. This is how you grow an unstoppable team.

A great leader has also mastered their ego, takes responsibility for everything that goes wrong, and gives credit to others for anything that goes right.

If this sounds like a lot, it's because it is. Being a great leader is a lifetime goal. In fact, it goes beyond your lifetime. Truly great leaders leave a legacy after they are gone. Remember the story of Walt Disney? His legacy of creativity has lived far beyond his lifetime. The Disney company is bigger and stronger than ever and has grown great leaders within its ranks, inspired by Walt's leadership.

Dr. Martin Luther King, Jr. was killed more than fifty years ago, but his influence is felt just as strongly today. And the list goes on.

TRUE LEADERSHIP

Being a leader means you are clear on your core beliefs. More importantly, those beliefs are nonnegotiable. True leaders do not compromise on their beliefs. Their beliefs are not situational or conditional. So the first powerful question becomes, "What do you believe that is unshakeable, that you'll never compromise on?"

Many people are put in a position of leadership, but that doesn't make them leaders. That only means they're in charge. They're the boss, the captain, or the coach. You can be in charge of a group of people, or even a whole company, and be a lousy leader. There are plenty of them out there. And every one of them lacks core values that are nonnegotiable.

Another thing great leaders seem to have in common, in my experience, is optimism. Now, throughout my career I've had people challenge this belief that you need to be an optimist to be a leader. People will proudly tell me, "I'm a realist," to which I reply, "Yeah, that's what all you pessimists say."

Being an optimist doesn't mean you see the world through rose-colored glasses. It means you have a vision that the world can be better and that you can make it better by your actions. All great leaders are visionaries who imagine something better. They imagine their product can be better, their people can be better, and they can be better.

An optimist is committed to being a problem-solver. A pessimist takes pride in pointing out the problem and often more pride in saying there is no solution. And they love being proved right. But what did they contribute? Negativity. Bravo.

A leader's positivity is driven by their optimism. They inspire people to be better, work harder, and chase their dreams because they are chasing a dream with persistence, determination, and the absolute belief they will find a way.

I'll give credit to pessimists for one thing: they are usually five times more accurate at seeing things as they are in the moment. But in my experience, through decades of observation, the optimists *succeed* five times as often. This is because an optimistic leader sees things as they are *and* sees how they can make them better. Most importantly, an optimistic leader never sees things as worse than they are.

A leader is not obsessed with the worst-case scenario. That takes too much energy and aims that energy in the wrong direction. As a problem-solver, a leader knows they will encounter problems and can only anticipate some of them. However, they have committed to solving the problems that appear rather than directing all their creative energy to imagining every possible thing that could go wrong.

Great leaders often have a pessimist by their side to do a reality check. This is so they don't get pulled down a negative path by having to focus on anything unnecessarily. But in my life, I've never seen a pessimist succeed greatly, and I've never seen a pessimist inspire people.

So it comes down to a few more powerful questions. Do you want to be right, or do you want to inspire people? Do you want to be right, or do you want to create something? Do you want to be right, or do you want to make a difference? You have to decide which of these is more important to you and which you think makes you a better leader.

Also, being right is an ego thing. It's not a leadership thing. A leader doesn't take any joy in being right because they predicted how bad things could go. A great leader sees failure as a challenge to try to solve a problem in a different way.

A true leader knows how to work with a team. They never believe they can do it all themselves—that's an ego trap. A great leader empowers others, and great leaders don't believe they have all the answers. If I said, "I succeeded all on my own," that would be my ego talking. But I know the truth, which is that I may be brilliant at a few things, but the reason I've succeeded to this level is that I've surrounded myself with brilliant people, most of whom are smarter than me.

A great leader has learned how to listen. There's no point in surrounding yourself with a great team if you're not going to pay attention to what they have to say. Collaboration is the way your dream and your vision become reality—perhaps an even greater one than you imagined.

As I said earlier, a great leader sees more in people than they see in themselves. Great leaders grow leaders. A very personal example for me is one of my team members, Kim McGuire, who started with me many years ago as my personal assistant. Today, she is the COO of our company. And I'm equally proud of the fact that both my daughter Jennifer and my son Michael have leadership roles in our business and are achieving great things and inspiring new ideas.

DECISIVENESS

Another attribute of leadership I have found to be crucial is decisiveness. Great leaders make decisions. They don't get trapped in analysis paralysis. They don't wait until they are certain of the outcome before acting. They don't obsess about perfection. They make decisions and act upon them, and they expect and encourage their people to do the same.

I had the great privilege of sharing the dais with General Norman Schwartzkopf a few years ago at a speaking event. You may recall him as the commander of the US forces during Desert Storm. When he spoke to the audience, he drove this single point home: with all the generals and leaders under him, he insisted they make decisions. They didn't always have all the information, but he didn't want them to only make decisions when they were certain of the outcome. That would be playing it too safe.

He let them know he understood they weren't always going to make the right decision. But he believed that even if they made the wrong decision, it just eliminated another path, so they would eventually get to the right decision. He even complained a bit about how the Pentagon would often get so mired in the process of trying desperately to determine the right decision that they would often become paralyzed, make no decision, and miss opportunities.

Schwartzkopf also said there's no possible way to always make the right decisions. No one can. But being a leader means deciding, acting, and learning. You don't obsess about blame when there is failure. You use the information to advance your situation and find a better path to your goals.

Great leaders grow leaders.

That's when Schwartzkopf pointed out to the other important quality of a leader. He said, "When in doubt, trust your true north." It's called integrity. It comes down doing the right thing, guided by your integrity. When you don't know what to do, trust your gut. Lean on your core values. The fact is, you can't always know what to do. No one can predict the future that accurately. But you can almost always dig into yourself and discover what you *should* do.

I'll come back to my point about a leader seeing more in people than they see in themselves. I have found that people will play up to their leader's high expectations. They will also play small, play safe, and play down to a leader's low expectations. If you want to grow leaders, it becomes imperative that you see more in them than they see in themselves.

Micromanagement is the opposite of having high expectations. It's lowering your expectations of people to the point where you effectively disempower them. You communicate mistrust in their capabilities. You demotivate them and eliminate their pathway to leadership.

Empower and inspire people, and motivate them to be the best they can be. That's great leadership.

POWERFUL QUESTIONS

- Am I an optimist?

- What core values do I have that are nonnegotiable?

- How important is it for me to be right?

- Do I tend to micromanage?

- Am I decisive?

21

TOUCH IT ONCE

THE TOUCH IT ONCE PRINCIPLE IS THE IDEA THAT WITH everything that comes across your desk, so to speak, you only deal with it once. You either handle it right then and it's done, or you decide who is going to own it.

This concept of touching it once comes directly from our discussion about an empowering leader. A disempowering leader micromanages. A great leader delegates.

When your operational principle is to touch it once, the ramifications are that you effectively delegate, showing your trust in people to make good decisions, all while eliminating redundancy in your business life. That way you can focus exclusively on the most important things you need to do.

I've already presented the idea that you don't manage time; you manage your energy. This puts that concept into everyday action. You are managing your energy by not doing something someone else should be responsible for and could even be doing better than you. And you are managing your own energy by not constantly monitoring the process.

Micromanaging is a huge energy drain. Touching it once moves 180 degrees from that, forcing you to ask if you should have any involvement at all in certain tasks. If you have the right people working for you—and again, this comes down to the leadership principle of making your people better—then you delegate responsibility.

Touching it once doesn't mean I'm never going to be involved in a project again. It means I've made a decision about who *owns* the project, and it's not me. I may be a constant resource for that project and provide input, but I've empowered someone else to manage the project and take full responsibility for it. This is how you grow people.

Micromanaging disempowers your people.

For example, we may design a new website. I sign off on the expenditure, and then someone else owns the project. They may email me at some point and ask, "Do you want your image on the home page?" I respond with a yes, and that's it. I don't check to see if the image is my favorite, if it's big enough, or if it goes with the background. I let someone else who knows websites better than me make those decisions.

On the surface it may look like I'm avoiding responsibility, but it's the opposite. My day is full. But it is filled with activities that require my full attention that only I can do and that almost always involve a singular task, not a repetitive one.

I came up with this approach because I am constantly asking this very important question: "Is this the best use of my time?" I realized long ago if I wanted to have a great impact on the world and be truly successful, I couldn't let myself get trapped in the minutiae. And so I found great people, grew them and empowered them, and finally came to the radical conclusion I could almost always touch everything just once. And it has worked.

Now, I work with my clients and my team to make sure they are asking the same question themselves, delegating what they should, and not getting trapped in micromanagement.

I have a side note on micromanagement. If it is not really your nature to micromanage and yet you find yourself doing it with a certain team member, you've got the wrong team member. Or at the very least, you've delegated the wrong project to them. If you can't touch it once, that should be a big red flag for you.

AVOIDING OVERLOAD

When I do lectures for groups of clients, I say I'm the CEO of Fortune Management, but I own nothing. Immediately the reaction is, "What do you mean you own nothing?" I pique their interest by putting it this way. Then I explain it is not my job to do repetitive processes. It is not my job to own assignments and projects. That's why I have brilliant people working for me. This way 100 percent of my energy goes to whatever will give me the highest-value result. None of my energy is wasted.

In the past, I often put myself in the position of overloading myself with responsibility. I made the buck stop with me on way too many things. I realized my productivity was a fraction of what it should have been. I was like a computer with too many programs running at the same time. My energy was dissipated.

My willpower would get drained as well, so I started taking things off my plate until everything was off it. Suddenly, I was much more effective. I had full energy for the most important things and none of the distraction.

If you don't find a way to release responsibility, it will follow you around. I'll give you a practical approach to solving that. In the many years my business was struggling, I wrote in a journal before I went to bed. I wrote everything I was concerned about that had emerged that day. I put it down on paper, and it released me from it. If you don't release it, what happens? You play it in a loop over and over in your head when you're lying there awake. Of course, you can't do anything about it in the middle of the night, but it wrecks your sleep.

What emerged from that was I not only started writing down the concern, but I began to also decide who could solve it or who could own at least certain parts of it. And more and more often, it wasn't me. I became creative and analyzed problems by figuring out who else could best handle the situation. Or I figured out who I needed to hire or grow so they could handle it and take it off my plate. If I couldn't find someone to own it, that told me I needed to hire someone new.

What evolved from that was I became vigilant about touching something once, offering guidance and support, and moving on to something that did require me to work on it. This was the highest use of my energy. And I got a good night's sleep on top of it.

I see so many people who believe they are the only ones smart enough to do everything in their business. (There's that ego again.) They need to have their fingers on everything. Everything needs to be run past them. They don't see they are so bogged down in the details that they are decades from achieving their dreams. And they don't see the impact it has on their people. People get discouraged when they are disempowered and frustrated they are never stretching themselves to get better because they haven't been given the room to do that. And very often, they leave. Especially the ones with the most potential.

Another tactical approach in touching it once came to me from a book called *Getting Things Done* by David Allen. This book taught me a couple of things. One was the "two-minute rule." It states that if you can get something done in two minutes or less, do it right now. The second thing I learned was that some things need incubation. Put them somewhere, such as a separate file in your inbox. Allocate time to review them, ponder them, and see who should own them.

But also, remember when we talked about no work, no play, just life, and we put all the items into two columns? All the tasks and things you don't want to do were on the right side. Imagine if you found a way to touch those things just once. How wonderful would life be? And all those things on the left, those things you love to do, that's what you touch continually. That's what you get better at. That's a life by design.

SHARPENING YOUR FOCUS

I've learned that my job is to lead. My job is to create and refine the vision for the company and deliver that message and knowledge whenever and however I can. When I walk on stage, I can't think about the ten different divisions of Fortune Management and the twenty-seven emails that popped up in my inbox. I need to be completely focused on giving that audience 100 percent of Bernie. When I coach a client on a major transaction, I want to be 100 percent focused on that deal. That's my highest, purest value.

Finally, a profound impact occurs because my people know I trust them. Please understand this. You can't leverage your time and energy if you don't leverage the talent and skills of your people. It's that simple. Touching it once is the ultimate solution.

POWERFUL QUESTIONS:

- What or who am I micromanaging?

- What am I not touching once?

- Are all my activities the best use of my time?

- What person or system needs to be put in place so I can touch everything once?

- When will I start?

22

BUILD A
PERSONAL BRAND

In business today, building your own personal brand is critical. This is in part because you may have ten different careers over the course of your lifetime, work for twenty different companies, and even change industries, but your brand will follow you wherever you go. The other reason is that if you're not consciously building your personal brand, it's being created without you in other people's minds.

Understand that when I talk about always being the best Bernie I can be, the direct result is that I'm building my personal brand. I am making a clear distinction between myself and other people, particularly those in the same field. So my advice remains: *always do you*. Don't try to do anyone else. Try to do the best you possible and make that as unique as possible.

What is a personal brand? At its core, it is a promise you make to your customers, your partners and your people. It's what you teach people to expect from you. Just like any other business, you need to build that brand. You need to define and refine that promise, and then communicate it effectively.

A personal brand is no different than a corporate brand. It establishes in people's minds what they can expect from you and what you're worth. Think about the value of a particular brand from a consumer product standpoint. Doesn't that brand influence your decision about whether to buy their product over someone else's? Doesn't that brand influence how much you're willing to pay for that product? Of course it does. People buy a Mercedes Benz because they have a brand expectation, and they know they are going to pay more for it. They also know if they buy a Kia, then they shouldn't expect a Mercedes level of quality, but they will pay a lot less.

Your brand is an accumulation of all your actions, successes and failures, and promises you've made, kept, and broken. For example, the win/win approach isn't just one of my principles. People have seen me walk away from a win/lose deal over and over, and it has become part of my brand promise. I don't just profess it. I live by it.

ELEMENTS OF YOUR BRAND

Many of the principles in this book will contribute to your personal brand.

If you believe in abundance, it becomes part of your brand. If you believe in scarcity, people will know that about you, and it will shape your brand.

If you always lead with you giving hand, it becomes part of your brand.

If you dress for success, you are shaping your brand. Just like a company spending a great deal of effort and money developing a logo and packaging, your appearance is creating a brand impression.

If you always bring Humor and a Smile, that's part of your brand. If you are dry and humorless, that's part of your brand.

If you are adamant about always creating a win/win, that becomes a big part of your brand. If you're aggressive in every negotiation, if you leave a trail of broken promises or economic wreckage, that's part of your brand.

Do you see how your beliefs create your brand? And please know it's not just the beliefs you espouse but whether or not you are truly living by them.

Your brand is what other people believe about you.

Another word for this is your reputation. But when you think about it like a personal brand, you are ascribing a tangible value to it. You are seeing it as a promise you have to uphold. It's more powerful. You may think your brand is what you say about yourself, but it's not.

My dad used to say, "The measure of marketing is not what you say about yourself. It's what others say about you." This goes double for your personal brand. It's not who you say you are. It's what others are willing to say about you. Your brand is created by how you live your core values.

Take a look at the personal brands of people around you. Are some of them negative? Now think about how hard it would be to change your mind about them and their brand. That is the power of a personal brand and also the risk in ignoring it.

Look at the brands of people like Elon Musk. His brand is that he is an extraordinary visionary, capable of executing on that vision over and over successfully. He's also known as a loose cannon. Does that make him less appealing, or does it make him unique? You only have to look at the price of Tesla stock to decide that one.

Like everything else, your personal brand is a choice. You decide what it's going to be based on how you live your core values, and how nonnegotiable they are. And don't expect it to happen overnight. I've worked damn hard for decades to build my personal brand.

PROTECT YOUR BRAND VALUE

If you are not building your brand intentionally, then people make assumptions, often because of their own biases. People fill in the blanks. If you've achieved a certain level of success and have an expensive car and a nice home, some people will assume you're a selfish jerk because they think all rich people are selfish jerks. But if they see you leading with your giving hand and walking away from win/lose deals, then you become the exception in their mind. Your brand overcomes their bias. That's the power of a great personal brand.

If your reputation is being created whether you like it or not, why not take control of that? Consciously build your personal brand. Don't let it happen unintentionally. Something else also happens when you deliberately craft your personal brand. It actually develops a monetary value. An extreme example would be someone like Kim Kardashian. Many people think she has no real achievements except building her personal brand. Yet that brand is worth millions.

Just like a corporate brand, part of your personal brand is about the value you put on it. If a stranger comes to you for free advice based on your years of experience and you give it to them, what value did you put on your time? Zero. You have told people you're not an expensive brand.

For example, some people will endorse any product as long as they get paid for it. They are riding their personal brand but diminishing it in the long run when they do that. But if you guard your brand value and don't let it become diluted, its value will keep going up. You can find terrific products or services you really think are best in class and only associate yourself with those. This enhances your personal brand, and you can also charge more for endorsing those products because you are so selective. You end up making more money and preserving your personal brand.

Your personal brand will give you tremendous credibility. If you keep your promises and live your values, there is really no limit to what you can achieve. People will invest in you. People will buy from you. People will partner with you. And you will get to choose what works for you in your life by design.

Finally, everyone in your company should know their own personal brand matters and reflects on the business brand and your personal brand as the leader. Therefore, everyone on your team has to share the same core values. They need to be aligned.

You must be vigilant about them upholding those values and ruthless in the protection of your brand by rooting out anyone who isn't willing to live up to those standards.

Your true personal brand is what people say about you and what they believe about you. Make it good. And guard it with your life.

POWERFUL QUESTIONS:

- What is my brand promise?

- Am I living my core values?

- Am I communicating my brand?

- Do I know what people say about me?

23

COMMON SENSE
AND STREET SMARTS

While I consider education to be important in a general way, what I've seen lead to success for me and most of the entrepreneurs I know is a strong level of common sense and street smarts. These are not innate qualities. They have to be learned. Think of them as your real-world education through a heightened awareness of the world around you. This teaches you how the world of business really works and how people react.

I didn't find formal education valuable. I didn't see how a deep understanding of algebra and calculus, for example, was going to make me successful. Perhaps this was because I started working at such a young age and was developing my street smarts so early. I sought knowledge where I needed it, and it didn't come from college.

This is not to say that higher education has no value. Depending on your career, it could be critical. For example, if you are becoming a medical professional, a rocket scientist, or a genetics researcher, you need to log some serious time in a university.

The problem occurs when a person believes their education is all that is required for them to succeed, particularly in business. Even when education is required for your career, you still need to be aware of the real world. You still need common sense. This is why physicians go into residency when they finish medical school. They need to see how to apply their knowledge and get a heavy dose of real-world experience.

Too often I see people get their MBA and believe they understand everything about business. Most of the time, I've found that belief to be out of balance. Certainly, it helps to understand how to use spreadsheets and do analysis and projections, but there needs to be some context. That context can only come from venturing into the world, getting dirty, and making mistakes. I may be biased, but I've never met an MBA grad who could sell. I've also never met an MBA grad who came out and started a business successfully based on their book-learning.

My observation is that people can often be book smart and street stupid. Education should teach you to "learn how to learn." It should teach you how to find the resources and information you need. It should exercise your brain in your formative years, but it's not the whole solution. In fact, relying solely on education can be a detriment because people believe they have all the answers and don't think they need to learn from the world.

AWARENESS

The greatest variable in your life will be other human beings. Their behavior will not always be rational or reasonable. This is why your awareness has to be dialed in at all times. Bill Gates recently said that in his estimation, awareness is even more important than intelligence. I have seen this borne out throughout my life in business. I've met people with extremely high IQs who don't have a practical bone in their body. They gravitated toward education because it came easily to them and made them feel good about themselves, but they never turned their awareness to the outside world. They didn't develop their common sense. Even worse, they became over-confident in their capabilities based on how much book learning they had done.

Don't get me wrong. I read five or six business books a year. I'm constantly learning and educating myself. But I'm doing it because I already have context. I'm trying to get better, and sometimes how other people see things and what they've learned gives me valuable insights.

Education should be the resource you turn to so you can fill in the blanks and enhance your street smarts. This is why a fully employed MBA program is much more valuable. Everything those students learn has context in the current business world, and they can decide if a teacher is out of touch or right on the money. They are in school but constantly aware of what real-world business problems entail.

I think common sense and street smarts are even more critical in today's rapidly changing world. Many students enter college with a career in mind, but by the time they graduate, that career is becoming obsolete, done by robots, software, or someone in India for a tenth of the money. Common sense and street smarts teach you to adapt and adjust to the accelerating shifts in the modern marketplace.

Developing awareness requires you to refine your sensory acuity. This means you don't jump to conclusions with the first bit of information. Observe and absorb. Be curious, and most of all, don't think you have all the answers.

LEARN FROM THE
REAL WORLD

What I see happen with book smart people is they get trapped in the theoretical. They develop beliefs about how things *should* work or what people *should* do. And I've watched that mindset crash on the hard rocks of reality.

There are some people who make the education system work because they don't fall into this trap. The author Brené Brown, who has written brilliant, insightful books on leadership, is a researcher at a university. That's her actual profession, but she has massive common sense and street smarts because her research looks at how people behave and react. She is constantly learning from the real world and translating that information into valuable, practical lessons and insights. Her sensory acuity is on full blast. She is not hiding behind the theoretical but instead building her theories from the street.

I've had people apply to work for Fortune after taking extensive coaching courses. They've never coached anyone, but they think they're ready. They're not. Others may be pretty good at coaching, but they can't convince anyone to be a client. Big problem.

If I'm adding someone to my team, my priority is evaluating if they have common sense and street smarts. They may have three degrees and have taken a multitude of advanced courses. But I want to know if they can interact with human beings, read them and influence them, and get real results in their coaching while dealing with their own failures.

If you're going to be an entrepreneur and invent a new way of doing things, you won't find the answer in a book. You'll find it by being keenly aware of what people need and want and working to create a solution.

If you're wondering why you're failing or you're worried that your education is not giving you the magical success you thought it would, ask yourself what you are missing. I'll bet it's an awareness of the real world, the actual marketplace. You haven't developed common sense because you didn't think you needed it. You just needed facts from books. And you didn't work on your street smarts because you actually look down on people who've developed them instead of going to school for sixteen years. You've got a bias, an experience problem, and an awareness problem.

DEVELOP YOUR SENSORY ACUITY

Bias and lack of experience or awareness are only problems if you allow them to stay that way. Step one for you, your first awareness challenge, is to realize that what you don't know or understand and what you're deficient in will never be fixed in class.

There's a term called the school of hard knocks. I'll take someone with that degree every time. I'm fine if they've got a significant education, but do they have business acumen? Do they have actual skills? They may be able to read a balance sheet, but can they tell what that balance sheet means? Can they interpret it and reveal the hidden deficiencies in the business? That comes with experience.

But don't just think experience is enough either. If you've got tons of experience but you're not paying attention, your sensory acuity is low. You're going nowhere.

Awareness is even more important than intelligence.

As always, ego is the inhibitor. Ego makes people gravitate toward more book learning so they can be "smarter" than the next person. It's what keeps them from developing street smarts because they need to believe they already know all they need to know. Suspend your ego and give your sensory acuity a chance to go to work. It will teach you what you need to know, develop your insights, and improve your capability to understand and influence people.

The ego also lets you tell yourself, "Hey, I have common sense. I've got street smarts," even when you don't.

You know who will tell you if you've got those ski

In the end, there's book smart and street smar both?

POWERFUL QUESTIONS:

- What do I rely on more, my education or r ence?

- How can I improve my sensory acuity?

- Do other people think I have common sen them!)

- Where do I go for answers?

- What is the real world trying to tell me that listening to?

24

TAKE A STAND

IF YOU'RE AN ENTREPRENEUR IN BUSINESS, THERE WILL BE times when you need to take a stand. Now, what are you taking a stand for? You could be taking a stand for yourself. You may be taking a stand for your brand. You might be taking a stand for integrity and what you know to be right. Or you might take a stand for other people in your company.

In some cases, that means you have to speak up or hold your ground. In other cases, it may be that you walk away from something, like a deal. It could also mean you inject yourself into a situation instead of sitting on the sidelines. If I find myself taking a stand on something, it's because I see a situation that appears to be going against my core values.

Often the hardest time to take a stand is when it matters most. The stakes are higher. Part of what prevents people from taking a stand when it matters is they don't believe in abundance. They believe if they miss out on an opportunity or they go against someone, the loss may be difficult to survive. Their beliefs are conditional. They are coming from scarcity.

Sometimes taking a stand will cost you money. It may also cost you a friend or someone you thought was a friend. It may cost you an opportunity. But here is why you do it. First of all, you need to have some values that are nonnegotiable. This is required to be leader, but it's also important for your personal brand.

If you espouse certain beliefs but aren't willing to make any sacrifices to uphold those beliefs, then people will learn they are just words. There's nothing behind it. If people figure out that I'll bend my win/win rule if the deal is lucrative enough, then what does my brand really mean? It means Bernie is for sale; you just need to figure out the price.

If you compromise your integrity once, it's a long road back.

You need to be willing to take a stand when your integrity is at stake. If you compromise your integrity even once, it's a long road back. And it becomes is a slippery slope where you find more and more rationalizations for why integrity doesn't matter in certain situations. And there goes your personal brand.

I think it goes even deeper than that. When you are willing to take a stand for something, you feel better about yourself. An essential part of a life by design is you have to like who you become and who you are becoming. Sometimes no one will know you took a stand except for you. But that's the point. *You* will know, and that's what matters most.

What many people do instead of taking a stand is they choose to "let it slide." That's avoiding difficulty and going easy on yourself. But it's also eroding your beliefs about yourself.

I'll give you a personal example. If I'm in a public place and I happen to see a father strike his child, I'm going to speak up. I'm not going to let it slide. I'm going to say, "Hey, buddy, calm down. Take a breath."

Most likely he's going to tell me to mind my own business. But in my mind, it *is* my business. He's teaching that child that violence is how your express your anger. And I don't want more people like that in my world. So I take a stand.

YOUR VALUES ARE YOUR GUIDE

Let's take this from personal to political. We have a rule in this country that we don't negotiate with terrorists. Not because we don't want a positive outcome but because we don't want to legitimize their behavior even one time because then the message is out there permanently that we will negotiate.

I transfer that same belief to business. If someone is trying to leverage their position with me by threats of any kind, then the negotiation is over. I don't mean physical threats, of course, but demands, blackmail (emotional or otherwise), and other similar behaviors. I'll take the consequences, but I'm not folding. It's win/win, or "Bye-bye."

You may find yourself in a situation where you have to fire an employee for legitimate reasons, and they tell you, "If you fire me, I'm going to sue you for wrongful termination." Now, your attorney may advise you to let them keep their job or to write them a big severance check. But you know what I say? I say, "Bring it." Because I don't negotiate with terrorists.

I've been in more than one legal conflict where my attorneys have advised me to just settle the matter. And there are certainly times when I do that because litigation is often a huge waste of time and energy. But there are also times when a principle is at stake. Someone is violating a promise they made to me. At that point, I want to send a message that I'm going to take a stand, even if it's going to cost me more in legal fees and maybe even risk that a judgment won't go my way.

You may think this contradicts the Influence questions that ask, "Do you want to be right, or do you want the best outcome? Do you want to be right or be in a relationship?"

There is no conflict. The test is simple. Does your ego want to take a stand, or is it a true violation of your core values? It's pretty clear right away. The wisdom to compromise is an essential life skill. But so is the fortitude not to compromise when your values are at stake.

No one can take away your integrity but you. That's important to remember. You always have a choice. Sometimes the consequences are severe. So be it. That's life.

POWERFUL QUESTIONS:

- What will I stand for, no matter the consequences?

- What is nonnegotiable for me?

- When have I compromised my integrity, and what has it cost me?

25

CHERISH
THE BRAND

IF YOU HAVE A BUSINESS OR YOU ARE WORKING FOR A BUSINESS, realize that the brand is more important than you. There is no better employee than one who cherishes the company brand, protects it, upholds it, reinforces it, and spreads its value to everyone they come in contact with.

And there is no wiser business owner than one who sees that the brand is more important than they are. This is true even when the founder has a strong personality. When Steve Jobs was alive, he was synonymous with the brand, but for everyone at Apple, including him, it was always about the brand, and a product had to fulfill the brand. You didn't see his photo on the billboards or the packaging. You saw the logo.

Take Disney again as an example. Walt was the creative visionary, but the brand was even more important. Everyone knew the Disney brand stood for wholesome family entertainment. Everyone knew that safety and cleanliness were paramount in the amusement parks. And because of that clear vision of what the brand meant, Walt could inspire his people to constantly expand and elevate the brand and what it offered. People didn't brag that they worked for Walt. They bragged that they worked for *Disney*. They cherished the brand. And they still do, long after he's gone.

We have a rule at Fortune that we adapted from the sports world. We say, "Don't let the name on the back of the jersey be bigger than the one on the front." In other words, you can be great at what you do, but always be subservient to the brand, the company. If you elevate yourself above the brand, your ego is starting to take over. Being the Best doesn't mean you are better than the company itself.

Another way to put it is the company's brand isn't you. It's everyone.

POWERFUL EXAMPLES

Tom Brady, the superstar quarterback, recently won his seventh Super Bowl. But if you were watching, you saw that when they handed him the trophy, he called all his teammates up to share in the glory, reminding everyone it was the Tampa Bay team that won. He didn't put himself above the brand. And if anyone could, it would be him. But he's wise enough to know he didn't do it all by himself. He was wearing a Buccaneers jersey.

In any business, when one individual believes they're bigger than the brand, it doesn't end well. Sometimes it even destroys the brand.

You see this happen with rock bands all the time. Look at the Beatles, who made some of the most enduring music in history. Put simply, John Lennon reached a point where he didn't cherish the brand, and it caused the breakup of the Beatles in less than ten years. And we can forgive Lennon because he was a young man. Who would have taught him to cherish the brand above all else?

But contrast that with the Rolling Stones, who are still together sixty years later. Mick Jagger could certainly have considered himself more important than the brand, but instead, he cherishes it. Look at U2, who, like the Beatles, were four teenagers getting together to make music. They're still together forty years later. Bono could have easily let his ego take over and say he was bigger than U2. But he didn't. He cherishes the brand.

Don't let your ego make you bigger than the brand.

I'm not saying you should blindly trust every brand out there. What you should do is find a company where you could cherish the brand if you worked for them, and you could also contribute to that brand.

I'm also saying that if you create your own business, never put yourself above the brand. As the CEO of Fortune, I'm at the forefront of the brand because I do a lot public speaking. But the brand means everything. When someone is carrying a Fortune business card, they're not representing me. They're representing the brand promise of Fortune Management. Twenty years after I'm gone, that brand promise will still be there because the people who work for Fortune cherish the brand.

This doesn't mean you aren't working on your personal brand when you cherish the company brand. In fact, it's the opposite. If you're working your way up the corporate ladder and everyone sees you are someone who cherishes the company brand, represents it well, and upholds its values and meaning, then you enhance your personal brand at the same time.

If you want something enduring, whether it's your own business or your personal brand, it's essential to cherish the brand you represent. Never allow your ego to say you are bigger than the brand.

POWERFUL QUESTIONS:

- Do I represent the brand promise well?

- Do I consider myself more important than the brand?

- What are good examples of brands that people cherish?

26

SET GOALS

THERE ARE MOUNTAINS OF BOOKS ON THE IMPORTANCE OF setting goals. The reason for that is simple. Without goals, you don't know where you're going. Let me refine that. Without *clearly defined goals,* you don't know where you're going, so the odds of your actions being in direct alignment with achieving them are slim.

There is an old saying that life will give you whatever you ask for. But the bottom line is, you have to ask for it. When you set a goal, you are asking a powerful question of the universe, so you'd better be precise in your request. A goal gives you something to play to, to aim your energy and focus at. If it's vague, you're going to waste a lot of time and energy.

I'll give a simple example. You may say your goal is to live in California. Okay, but where in California? By the beach in Santa Monica? In the mountains of the Sierras? In farm country?

Those are entirely different places. You could cross the line from Nevada and be in California, but you could find yourself in a barren desert. Did you reach your goal?

Many people say one of their goals is to be rich. What could be more vague? How rich? How much money do you need to be financially free and live the lifestyle you want? And, more importantly, what exactly does that lifestyle look like? That's what you should be asking.

Setting goals is about dreaming greatly. Goals should stretch you, take effort, and maybe even seem impossible right now. They should excite you. You've only got one life, and the clock is running.

THE SUCCESS FORMULA

Remember our formula for ultimate success—those five steps that delineate goals and create a path to reach them? Let's break it down again.

1. Know your outcome. That's the goal itself, as clearly and precisely as you can define it.

2. Know your Why. This defines the passion you have to achieve the goal and what motivates you to get there.

3. Take massive action. Not casual action. Not occasional action. Setting the goal doesn't get you there by itself. You need to act.

4. Monitor and measure your results. Are your actions moving you directly toward your goal?

5. Change your approach as many times as necessary. You will be learning every step of the way, and the goal itself will need to be refined, or your course of action may need to pivot.

These steps apply to any goal you want to achieve, whether personal or professional. If you want to be a great parent, what does that look like? Does it mean your children have successful careers? Why is that important to you? What will you do to make sure that happens? How much money will you need for their education? How will you gauge success along the way? What needs to be adjusted in your parenting as time goes by and as each child's unique personality emerges?

When I talk to clients about their goals, they tell me they want to be wealthy, healthy, and happy. To me, those aren't answers. Those aren't goals. I am adamant about them being laser-focused on what they're truly aiming for and why.

Let's use wealth as an example. Significant research has shown that after around $75,000 a year of income, any increase beyond that doesn't equate to a proportional increase in happiness. I've seen this myself. I know multimillionaires who are in a constant state of stress and anxiety because they're worried they won't be able to sustain their income, or worse, it's not enough because their friends make even more than they do. I also know people who make $80,000 a year and are completely content. Money doesn't equal happiness in direct proportion. Wealth is relative.

When a client tells me that they want to make a million dollars a year, I ask them why. They might say, "So I can live the lifestyle I want." I then ask, "Why do you want that lifestyle, and what does that exactly look like?" I dig deeper and deeper until they can be precise about that lifestyle. They may want to travel one month out of every year. They may want to donate a month of their time to a favorite cause. They may want their kids to be able to go to medical school. Now the goal is becoming clearly defined.

BE CLEAR AND PRECISE

When you define the lifestyle precisely, you can also get smarter about how much wealth you really need to achieve it. For example, some people's lofty goal is to only fly on private jets. Do they need to own a jet? A Gulfstream G550 costs $60 million, with annual operating costs of around $1.5 million. How much flying are you really going to do? Maybe just booking a private jet when you want would be a fraction of that. Maybe you just need friends who own jets.

This thinking can be applied to every aspect of your desired lifestyle.

When you design a goal with laser focus, you can plan a course of action. Knowing clearly why you're doing something will pull you toward that goal, giving you the real motivation you need. The clearer the dimensions of your goal, the easier it is to take massive action in the direction of your goal.

The more clearly defined your goals are, the easier they are to monitor. Let's say one of your goals is to be healthy. You know what I'm going to say, right? That's not clear enough. So now you define specifically what healthy means to you. For example, you want to be able to run five miles comfortably. You want your body mass index to be twenty. You want to keep all your teeth as long as possible. Do you see how getting precise in the details of your goals makes your progress measurable?

When I am setting goals with clients, I always ask, "Where are you right now?" Then I ask, "How did you get to this point in your life?" Then I ask them where they want to be at a certain point. I remind them the past does not equal the future, and what got them to where they are may not get them to where they want to go. When they decide exactly what that goal looks like, then they can make an action plan, which may be radically different than what they've done before.

Now comes the important part for you in your achievement of any goal. What are you doing every day to make progress toward that goal? The more daily actions you take, the more you inch toward that goal or even fulfill it. When you make your massive action plan, spell out what you will do every day, every week, and every month toward that goal, with an emphasis on every day.

PROGRESS AND REFINEMENT

As you get older, years go by like minutes. I've observed that if you don't put your focus on a goal for some part of your day and take some action, suddenly that dream slips away. That's why I start every day looking at my life wheel and what I'm going to do in each area to keep aligned with my goals.

Very often I see people espouse certain goals, but they aren't making much progress toward them, and they wonder why. In every case, it's because their daily actions are out of alignment with their goals. Or they don't even have the steps laid out.

If you say you want to be economically free but you spend every penny you make, you are out of alignment with your goal. If you say you want to be the best oral surgeon in your city but you only take one or two clinical courses a year and focus way more on your golf game, then you are out of alignment. And you know what I see as the result? You're not happy.

The past does not equal the future.

When your actions are aligned with your goals, then the journey itself becomes satisfying. This is a powerful thing to understand. The joy comes with the journey more often than reaching the goal because every day is satisfying. What's more, you will constantly need to adjust your goals because if you are applying CANI, then you will get better and better at achieving them, and you'll have to dream bigger.

Let's go back to the person who wanted to travel one month out of every year and donate a month of their time every year. They may reach a point of economic freedom and realize, "I'm bored with travel. After a week I just want to be back home." So they adjust. They also realize that when they work with Habitat for Humanity, it's the most satisfying part of their year. So now they do it for three months each year.

REFINE
YOUR GOALS

Our goals mature over time, so we refine our skill of achieving any goal we have. But understand you may not reach your goal exactly on schedule or in exactly the same way you designed it. I have an expression I use, which is, "God's delays are not God's denials."

This is my way of reminding myself and other people that we won't always understand the grand design that exists for our lives, but as we become more aware and refine what finding our fortune really means, we will arrive somewhere glorious. But not always on our timetable.

I urge you to have clear goals for every element of your life wheel. They are all important. Some of them may take more thought to clearly delineate. For some, the actions themselves are the goal. Take spirituality, for example. Your goal may be to pray every day and attend weekly gatherings in your house of worship. Or you may just want to meditate every day. Or you could define your spirituality as generosity and donate 10 percent of your income to charity. You define what your spirituality looks like, and then you take daily action.

Relationships are the same. You can clearly define how you will be with your significant other. It could be something as simple as always having date nights or bringing them coffee in the morning. It may be that you work to understand their love languages and make an effort to fulfill one or more of them every day. Once again, just saying, "I want to be a good spouse," is not a clearly defined goal. How could you measure that?

THE TIMING
OF GOALS

This leads to an understanding of the timing of goals. Some may take years or decades to reach. Some may be annual, like what we do with our dental clients at Fortune. Some may be weekly, like your exercise regimen, and others may be daily, like meditation.

When we do our annual planning with our Fortune clients, it's a time of monitoring and recalibration. Then we decide how far we can stretch in the next year and get everyone aligned on the actions they will be taking, week by week. I sincerely believe this process is why many of our clients consistently grow their revenue by 30 percent or more every year. This whole process is proven and powerful.

The other reason you want to be skilled at setting and reaching your goals is the effective pursuit of happiness. Human beings are happiest when they are doing two things: growing and contributing. When you incorporate goal-setting skills into your life and execute them this way, you will always be growing, and your contribution to your life, your family, your business, and the world will grow as well.

It truly becomes a life by design. The more precise you are in each aspect of your life, the more satisfying and fulfilling that life will be.

POWERFUL QUESTIONS:

- Are my goals clearly defined, with laser-like focus?

- Why do I want to achieve those goals?

- What are my clear goals for every aspect of my life wheel?

- What actions will I take in order to reach those goals?

27

PUT YOUR BUTT
ON THE LINE

Setting goals is critical to success. But here's what I've learned in my own life: in the end, to cement that success, you've got to put your butt on the line. You have to make a public declaration of your goals.

You can set clear goals, go through all the processes I talked about in the last chapter, and have a powerful why and an action plan. But one of the big mistakes people make is they keep all their hopes, dreams, and goals buried inside themselves. They're buried in their heart, their soul, and their brain. Many also just write them down.

The problem with that is, who's going to hold you accountable? One of the things I learned very early in my business career was to not be afraid to make a series of public commitments. Whenever I thought something was important enough for me personally, in my career, or for the company as a whole, I declared that goal publicly. That extra step makes all the difference and provides extra motivation to keep stepping up no matter how hard things get.

When I'm doing goal-setting workshops, first I get participants to write all their goals down. I make sure they have written clear goals for each area of the life wheel. I want them to go into great detail, but then I ask them to create a one-word or one-sentence summary of each of those six goals.

Then I say, "Let's add one more goal, which will be the reward for reaching these goals. Some nice vacation with the family or a team event in Las Vegas." I leave it up to them.

Then I tell them to take that list of seven goals, make several copies, and put them everywhere—on the dashboard of their car, on the bathroom mirror, on the refrigerator. I also tell them to carry the list around with them in their wallet or purse.

Now we get to the most important part. I say, "You need to tell everyone these goals. You need to publicly declare them. Let people know what you intend to do, and even ask them to hold you accountable. Get their support."

How many people have goals in their lives but don't even spell them out to their life partner? It mystifies me. Some people say, "Well, I'm not sure they would support me in those goals." Well, that seems like a bigger problem of alignment, doesn't it? All the more reason to get it out in the open.

So tell everyone your goals. Let your team know you plan to grow revenue by 30 percent this year. Let them know you're going to lose twenty pounds by the end of the year. And the closer they are to you, the more you can spell out the clear steps you're going to take toward your goals.

Tell all your friends. Tell your family. Tell that nosy neighbor you see in the driveway every morning, the one who's going to ask you how you're doing with your diet. Why does this step scare people? It scares them because now they've got to truly commit. People don't like being embarrassed, so this declaration can provide the extra motivation to drive past McDonald's and grab a salad instead, stay an extra hour at work making calls until you find a new client, or practice the guitar instead of watching TV.

You will always need motivation to tap into the path to your goals. When you put your butt on the line, your reputation and your credibility are also at stake, so you'll go the extra mile.

CHUNKING YOUR GOALS

Achieving any goal comes down to chunking, which is breaking it down into daily or even hourly actions toward that final achievement. Putting your butt on the line gives you that extra boost to get to that action every day. If you've told someone you're going to hit the gym four days a week, it's a lot harder to let yourself off the hook than if you keep that goal private.

Most important, realize that what you do every day aggregates. Break the steps down as small as you need to so you can always get to them. That way you're not overwhelmed by the size of the goal. You've chopped it up into bite-sized chunks. As they say, a journey of a thousand miles begins with a single step. Break down the steps and start taking them, one by one.

When we plan goals with our dental clients for their production for the next year, we break it down not by month or by week but by day. We want that team to understand what they need to produce each day to hit that annual number. That's measurable, and it keeps you from drifting too far off course before you notice. The same thing applies to any of your goals.

Break your big goals down into bite-sized steps.

Making a public commitment can also drive your creative juices to figure out how you're going to achieve that goal when you're not sure ahead of time how you're going to get there. With my business, I often make a bold declaration of some new initiative that we're going to accomplish in the coming year. We may not know at the time how we're going to pull that off, but because of that public declaration, we've got to figure it out, step by step.

A goal pulls you even harder when you've made a public commitment. It's one of the great leverage tools you can use on yourself and with your company.

One last thing. When I have a goal I've set for myself, I visualize myself already achieving it, already in that place I want to be. I'm walking, talking, and living as if I've already reached that goal. It's incredibly empowering. Making a public declaration of that goal only amplifies that.

POWERFUL QUESTIONS:

- Who do I need to declare my goals to?

- Have I broken down my goals into small, achievable steps—ideally daily ones?

- Can I imagine myself already having achieved those goals?

28

MANAGING
YOUR STATE

EARLIER IN THIS BOOK, I TALKED ABOUT THE NEED TO DEVELOP emotional fitness and mental toughness. These are the results of effectively managing your state. It starts with understanding how powerful your mind is. You're capable of producing the endorphins you need, like serotonin, dopamine, and norepinephrine, and changing your physiology merely by changing how you think. Chemical reactions are going occur no matter what, and you can determine if they are fight or flight or uplifting by the state you choose to be in.

Here's a simple example of that. Remember the chapter about Humor and a Smile? The science shows we elevate our mood by choosing to put a smile on our face. It triggers a whole different flow of biochemicals than if we're frowning; it doesn't matter if we're in a good mood or not.

Managing your state is about controlling your reactions to get the results you desire. If you can't control your reactions and adjust your attitude, you won't be effective at influencing people. If you can't control your anger or your frustration without expressing it the moment you feel it, then your leadership will suffer and your relationships will suffer—and eventually, so will your health. Managing Your state means you rule your emotions rather than letting them rule you.

EMOTIONAL MASTERY

Emotional mastery starts by understanding you always have a choice. You may feel anger, but you don't have to express it. This comes down to simple behavioral changes, like pausing before you react. Then, you take the time to Speak from Intention. Ask yourself if expressing rage is going to get the outcome you're looking for. Probably not, in most instances. So hit the pause button. Take a few breaths.

Be keenly aware of this fact: every word that comes out of our mouths either pushes people away or brings people toward us. Mental toughness requires you to contain your response so you can be clear on your intention before you express yourself. Otherwise, you're just a reactor.

Managing your state at a level of mastery means you are consciously choosing the best state to be in at all times. You are choosing the emotions you express in every moment. As difficult as this may sound, once you believe it can be done and start doing it, suddenly how you feel throughout the day will change.

In my case, as I mentioned early on, I choose to come from gratitude, abundance, kindness, and happiness. You are free to choose where you come from because it is your design. But I recommend you make them positive emotions. You can choose to come from confidence and love every day. Or pride and generosity. It's your life. How do you want to feel? That's up to you.

Some people will immediately respond to this and say, "Yeah, but when I see someone toss a cigarette butt on the sidewalk, it makes me angry!"

Every reaction you have is a choice.

And I will ask, "Does it *make* you angry, or do you *let* it make you angry?" Saying that something "makes you" feel anything implies you are not in control. Saying, "I can't control how I feel!" is a massively false limiting belief. It's simply not true.

Developing emotional fitness and mental toughness means you've decided to always be in control. Do I ever want to feel angry? No. It doesn't feel good. So I decide to feel grateful instead. You can't feel angry and grateful at the same time. Grateful wins every time if you make that choice.

So how can I be grateful instead of angry when I see someone toss a butt on the ground? Simple. I can be grateful I don't let nicotine control my life. I can be grateful I don't waste all that money on cigarettes. I can feel empathy for this person's addiction and the fact that it makes them not care if they litter or not or that they're killing themselves. It's all about choices.

You can do this same thing in any situation, no matter how intense your emotion. It won't happen overnight, and you'll still be human. You'll feel fear, frustration, hurt, and betrayal. But you'll learn to handle it. Ask yourself powerful questions like, "What's good about this?" or "Is this an emotion I want to let control me?"

SUSPEND YOUR EGO

Managing your state also involves the strength and wisdom to suspend your ego. Your ego is where your strongest and often most unhealthy reactions will come from. When you recognize that, you can apply the wisdom to recognize what result you want and reverse engineer what you're going to say and how you're going to react. Then you are in control. Behavior equals results. Plain and simple. When you have the emotional and mental discipline to apply that wisdom, success will flow from it in every aspect of your life.

Your mindset, your beliefs, and the way you manage your state will be the major determining factors in reaching your goals and becoming the person you most want to be. If your mental state indicates you don't have the capability to do something, then your brain checks out. It coasts because you've set the limit. But when you have a mental state that is positive, optimistic, bold, and confident and that believes more is possible, then the brain starts to look for solutions.

I've seen this throughout my career coaching professionals. We don't just tell them the systems they need to apply and the practical adjustments they need to make in their business. That only makes a small difference. Because we start with their mindset, get them to recognize their limiting beliefs, and show them how to manage their state and build emotional fitness and mental toughness, suddenly their dreams get bigger. They reach those dreams because they have the formula.

Now you do too. And you can apply it to every area of your life wheel.

POWERFUL QUESTIONS:

- What results do I want, and how well do my reactions align with those results?

- Am I in control of my reactions when encountering difficult situations?

- Do I believe that I always have a choice in how to react?

29

EMBRACE
YOUR PAIN

I HAVE REACHED A PLACE IN MY LIFE WHERE I'M ACTUALLY thankful for the mistakes that have caused me pain at various times. That may sound crazy, but I've learned that pain is the greatest teacher we have. Think about the nature of human beings. What do we learn from most, success or failure? The painful truth is we learn a heck of a lot more from failure. Failure is full of useful information. Success could just mean we got lucky, our timing was good, or our competitor fell short.

Success is wonderful. It gives you something to celebrate. But I have learned to embrace pain. I've learned to welcome it. I am grateful for the time I lost over a million dollars in the restaurant business because it forced me to reassess and do a major course correction in my life.

I had reached a point back then where I had developed Midas Touch Syndrome. I was successful in every business I tried, so I believed no matter what I did, it was going to pay off. I believed I couldn't fail. Until I did. Big time.

I was forced to reflect on my pursuit of get-rich quick schemes and the emptiness of those successes. And even then, I had the mental toughness not to despair. I asked, "What is the message here? What's the lesson?"

I could have easily gotten depressed, angry, or suicidal even. I could have found several people to blame instead of myself. But that would have taught me nothing. Instead, I came to the realization I wasn't doing purposeful work, so it didn't matter if I succeeded financially or not. This led me to a career of teaching personal development, and it saved me. I now had real purpose behind my actions.

This is an example of embracing the pain on a large scale, but it applies to your everyday life as well, and every aspect of your life wheel. If you are continually in pain in your personal relationships, what is the reason? Blaming the other person won't help. You need to learn something about yourself, and you need to figure out what that is.

This can apply to your financial situation, health, career, spiritual life, and certainly emotional state.

My advice is don't wait until the pain gets bigger. I've come to believe the universe will keep turning up the volume until you listen. I could have figured out much earlier that my business endeavors had no real purpose except to give me money to indulge myself. But I didn't hear the message, so I believe the universe said, "Okay, maybe losing a million dollars might snap him out of his delusions."

The ego always wants to deflect the blame onto someone else. And often it appears that someone or something else is at fault. But until you embrace your pain by taking responsibility for it and reflecting on it, your life won't get better. You won't improve.

MISTAKES
CREATE INSIGHTS

Ray Dalio, in his marvelous book *Principles,* lays out a simple formula: Pain + Reflection = Evolution.

I love this formula. It encapsulates the whole idea of embracing your pain because until you are willing to reflect on your personal role in the mistake and try to find a deeper meaning whenever possible, you will be stuck in the same place, forced to repeat the mistake.

I see the most successful businesses consciously embrace failure as a learning process. Some of them even apply a principle of failing fast. They "fail upward," knowing the key is to just make the mistakes survivable.

Other companies punish failure, but that stifles innovation. Why would you take any risk if you'd be fired if your idea didn't work? If you create a culture like that, people are going to hide their mistakes.

The smartest companies I know reward mistakes and punish hiding them. They know the danger of people hiding mistakes, especially in a world where you need to keep adapting your business model every year or you're toast.

At Fortune we have a system we recommend to our clients where the company keeps a journal, and anyone who makes a mistake has to enter it into the journal. This way, the team can review the mistakes in their weekly meeting. It may show a flaw in the workflow or some training that everyone needs because they all would have made the same mistake in that situation. It's a learning tool. No one gets punished for the mistake as long as the intent was to try to make something better for the practice or the patient. But they are punished for hiding a mistake.

Ignoring the pain misses the message.

Here's the thinking behind this: when someone doesn't share their mistake, they are depriving the company of the chance to improve, to make everyone better. To ignore the pain and always punish screw-ups is a primitive approach and poor leadership. And the company will suffer in the end.

No matter how good you become at your business or your life, you will still make mistakes. There's no avoiding it, so why not embrace it? Why not make it meaningful and productive instead of something to be embarrassed about?

I'll tell my people all the mistakes I've made so they don't have to experience the learning firsthand. For example, I'm never going to invest in a company again just because the idea sounds good. I'm going to dig deep into that whole company plan and know the people who are executing it. Why? Because I've lost plenty of money when I haven't done that. I don't want people I know to make the same mistake.

Sometimes the pain can be subtle. I can find myself making a point I've made for years, and suddenly I notice it's not resonating. Maybe I'm using an analogy that my audience is too young to understand. (I'm sixty-three now. I remember the Brady Bunch!) It stings when I find myself not connecting, so I take a hard look at that particular message and see how it needs to be refined or even abandoned. I reflect on that sting so I can always be improving.

One of the worst things that can happen to you is getting so good at deflecting the cause of the pain that you're totally desensitized to it. Then you won't change and grow at all, and gradually that part of your life will get worse. It happens in relationships all the time, where someone loses touch with how they are making their mate unhappy. Typically, they make it the other person's problem. "Oh, he's just overreacting." "She doesn't appreciate my sense of humor." That's just avoiding embracing the pain.

When you are causing someone else pain so often you don't notice, you're in a tough spot. And the universe is going to turn up the volume on you. Don't let this happen to you. Reflect. Change.

I see a parallel in businesses where a person's income is in steady decline. They will dismiss it and say, "It's not serious. It's only five percent a year." I find myself pointing out that in four years they'll be down 20 percent, and that happens to be their entire profit margin.

The skill is to be tuned into the pain at work, in relationships, and even in your own body. Humans get stronger through adversity and challenge. I wouldn't be the man I am today if it weren't for all the pain that came my way. I'm grateful for it. And I will always embrace it and plumb it for its deepest meaning.

POWERFUL QUESTIONS:

- What are some of the most painful moments in my life or career?

- What are the lessons I could learn from them?

- Do I create a safe place for people to admit their mistakes?

- Do I embrace failure or avoid it at all costs?

30

EVOLVE

The rule in business, now more than ever, is evolve or die. That's the name of the game. If everything you're doing, whether it be in your company or your career, is exactly the same as it was ten years ago, you are in big trouble.

Remember Ray Dalio's formula, pain plus reflection equals evolution? When you embrace your pain, it lays the groundwork for the evolution of your business, your career, and your personal life.

Just as you need to embrace your pain, to evolve you need to embrace change. You need to learn and adapt new behaviors, new systems, and new approaches. You must be willing to let go of things that once worked for you because times have changed, the marketplace has changed, or your significant other has changed.

As important as it is to be constantly learning, it is also critical to be *unlearning*. To truly follow *kaizen*, you need to release old beliefs as you adapt new ones. For example, you may think social media is a stupid waste of time, but the reality is that's where you're most likely to find your customers nowadays. You need to embrace it whether you like it or not. Your judgment about it is irrelevant.

Evolving also brings in Embracing Technology. I'll often hear dental clients complain they don't want to adopt new technology because integrating it will slow them down. I try to remind them that what will really slow them down is a little thing called going out of business. Sometimes you have to slow down to speed up. Evolution isn't always comfortable or easy. In fact, it seldom is.

I encounter clients who have team members complain about how everything is always changing or that things are changing too fast. Sorry, but we live in a world of exponential change. Digging your heels in and resisting change is a pathway to unemployment for a team member, just as it is disastrous for a business owner. If you only want to work in a business that never changes, plan on looking for another job in five or ten years because that business will be gone.

START WITH YOUR MINDSET

The great teacher Jim Rohn, from whom I learned so much about personal development, would say, "If you want your life to be better, then you've got to get better." He drove home that the responsibility is on *you* to evolve, not for the world to adapt to you. That lesson stuck with me, and we incorporated it into the fabric of Fortune Management. All of us are trying to get better, and we're all coaching our clients on how to get better.

Jim would also point out that it doesn't take a lot to change yourself, and it doesn't take a long time. You just have to change your mindset. Change how you look at something, and then the change happens—often in an instant.

One example of this is when a cigarette smoker suddenly has a newborn child. They quit smoking that day and never smoke again. Think about that. They didn't learn anything new about the dangers of smoking. They just thought about it completely differently, that they were endangering their child. And their behavior changed that day.

Change your mindset, and you will change your life in that moment.

The challenge is when you want your life to be better, but you don't want to change anything. Well, if your current approach to everything was working perfectly, then you wouldn't need your life to be better, would you? But I'm guessing there are several ways you want your life to be better.

Not changing is stagnation. That doesn't equate to things just staying the same, by the way. It means things are slowly, steadily getting worse. There is forward or backward in life and in business. No neutral. Evolve or die.

SAVOR THE STRUGGLE

I'm convinced if you want your business to be around five years from now, you must evolve. This applies even if you're working for someone else. If they're doing business the same way they did ten years ago, you should probably be looking for another job. If you look closely at every business you see struggling, it's because they haven't changed. They're clinging to an old way of doing things and sitting back, waiting to be obsoleted.

And of course, with the 2020 pandemic, change and disruption were accelerated. There were way more winners and losers than in a typical year. And it always came down to step five in the Ultimate Success Formula, which is to always be adjusting and changing your approach.

If you want life to be better, you must get better.

For example, the restaurants that survived in 2020 pivoted completely to doing takeout. Some of them found they could make even more money that way than serving indoors. In my industry, if dentists didn't figure out how to adopt new safety procedures in their practices, they found a significant percentage of their patients migrating to practices that did adapt. Always be monitoring results and changing your approach. It's the only way to survive and thrive.

Evolution applies to your relationships as well as your business. How many people stay in lousy marriages because they're afraid to change, to go through the painful evolution that comes with breaking free and being on their own? How many people find themselves growing apart but don't do anything to fix it? It's one of the most important parts of your life wheel, so why wouldn't you be eager, determined even, to make it better? And the way you'll make it better is to be better. Evolve.

Here's another secret about evolution, and I mentioned this in the previous chapter. Human beings thrive and grow in adversity. When we are not challenged, we tend to coast, to stagnate, to get comfortable with the status quo. Adversity jump-starts us into action. It's a survival mechanism. So why not push yourself, challenge yourself, so that you're always evolving? Learn to savor the struggle. Put yourself in uncomfortable situations. Get out of your comfort zone. Learn something new. Why wait for the universe or the marketplace to come along with some unexpected adversity? Strengthen that change muscle ahead of time so you can adapt to whatever comes.

When you commit to evolving, your life becomes like water: you'll always find a way. When water is heading from the mountains to the ocean, it always finds a path, either over, under, or around. It will even build a lake until it has enough pressure to make a waterfall, and then away it goes again toward the ocean. You can be the same way, always trying a different approach, knowing where you're going and what your purpose is, and adapting and evolving every step of the way.

Finally, to tie this once more to another key concept, if you want to evolve, put your butt on the line. Make a public commitment to embrace change. And make those declarations specific. In fact, make it a core value of your business and your life to embrace change and always be evolving.

And then flow like water toward your dreams.

POWERFUL QUESTIONS:

- How have my beliefs changed over the years?

- What beliefs are holding me back?

- Where might I be stagnating?

- How has my business approach changed?

- Do I embrace change?

31

CHOOSE YOUR MEANING

LET ME PRESENT ANOTHER PROFOUND TRUTH: NOTHING HAS any meaning in our life except the meaning we decide to give it. This is based on the fact that nobody knows what reality truly is. I have my view of the world, and you have yours. Everyone has their own view of the world. Who's to say which is the correct reality? It's all interpretation. When you understand this, you can make choices about that interpretation. You can choose your meaning for any experience.

This is a complex concept, so I'm going to give you a simple example to start with. Someone cuts you off on the highway, and you say to yourself, "What a jerk!" Maybe you even honk your horn. You get a little angry. You've ascribed a meaning to the event along with a judgment about the person. Is that person really a jerk? You don't even know him. Is he even behaving like a jerk?

Maybe he's rushing to the hospital because his wife is about to have their first baby. Maybe if he's late for work he's going to be fired. Maybe he's so distracted he didn't even see you.

Do you see how many meanings there could be? So my advice to you in all situations is to choose a meaning that empowers you, controls your emotional state, and improves the relationship with that individual. Open your mind to other possibilities, and don't be attached to your reaction. Remember, when it comes to managing your state, you want to be in control of your emotional response. Choosing a meaning that is more positive makes that a whole lot easier.

This starts with understanding human nature. We are very good at jumping to conclusions. We are masters of having opinions with very little information to back them up. It's the way our brain works. If we don't have a lot of information, we turn to our biases, our prejudices, and our preconceived notions, along with our mood at the moment.

With that guy who cut you off, if you were having a bad day, you might have ended up flipping him off. Also, if he were driving a BMW, you might have had a totally different reaction than if he were driving a little pink Fiat. And if you were in a great mood, you might have just smiled, waved him in, and given him a thumbs up. Same event. Totally different reactions.

One final point about this situation. If he actually was a jerk, do you think he would care if you were angry about getting cut off? Not at all. So now you've got anger inflaming your body because of your choice of meaning. Your choice hurt you. Only you.

We have to be very careful about the meanings we assign to interactions and experiences because of the effect they have on us. I believe choosing the best meaning is one of the most powerful life skills you can develop. There is no part of your life wheel this won't affect, often in a powerful way.

THE REALITY CHECK

I'm going to give you a systematic way to choose the meaning that is most beneficial to you, so your reaction creates the best result. In my business we call it a Reality Check because you're admitting your version of reality is not necessarily correct, or maybe just not helpful to your state. Naturally, the system involves asking powerful questions.

Question 1: Do I want to make this situation better?

That could mean you want to feel differently, or it could mean you aren't heading toward the outcome you're looking for.

This is a defining question. If you say yes and it's about what you're feeling, now you are managing your state, and you know you need to choose a meaning that will change your state to one you want to be feeling. If you say yes and it's a business situation, now you need to focus on the outcome and not just react. You want the relationship to improve, the customer to be happy, or the deal to get done. You are shifting from urge to intention.

Let's go back to how you want to feel. If this is triggering a negative emotion, then you should want to change that. If you don't, then the larger question becomes why are you attached to that feeling? Are you saying you want to feel good about feeling bad? Then you've got some issues to deal with.

You will encounter people in life who actually behave this way consistently. They are attached to a world view that leads to a negative expectation about everything, so their reactions are not their fault. They don't believe they have a choice. This is a recipe for unhappiness. This is not a rich life.

Question 2: What meaning did I assign to the situation?

Did you come to a conclusion that said, "I can't trust this person," or "This person only cares about themselves"? How about, "This is the worst thing that's ever happened to me"? No matter what has occurred, you need to honestly define what interpretation you've given to the situation. Your reaction may be anger, frustration, disappointment, or even depression. You had to give a specific meaning to what happened for you to feel that. Get clear on the meaning.

Question 3: Do I have enough information to come to a conclusion?

How fact-based was your reaction? As someone famously said, there are always three realities: yours, mine, and the truth. When people say, "There are always two sides to a story," they are missing out on the third one. The two sides are opinions formed by each person's perspective.

You may not have nearly enough information to come to a conclusion, yet you've formulated an emotional reaction. Or you may have a lot of information, but it's coming through your filters. What information is the other person operating from? What's their reality? What filters might they be using?

Question 4: What else could this mean?

This is a life-changing question. It is liberating in a profound way because it frees you from believing your single interpretation is the right and only one. The process of reflecting on other meanings makes it possible for you to open your mind to a more positive choice, and very often a more accurate meaning.

You're now reexamining what you've revealed to yourself in Question 2. This gives you a very potent perspective, because if you can think of what else the situation could mean, you are on a path to discovering a way to react differently.

Let's say someone said something really harsh and hurtful to you, and you decide they are a mean person. What else could it mean? Maybe they were just having a bad day. Maybe they had something else going on in their life that made them treat you that way. Maybe the other person was doing their best with what they had available to them at that moment, and maybe they felt close enough to you that they could overreact without you judging them too harshly.

Do you see all the options, all the choices? One of the greatest things you can do when a human being treats you poorly is to pause and wonder what's going on with them. Maybe it's not about you at all.

Too often, we want to make it all about us. It's not always about us. People are living lives we don't know about. This fourth question challenges you to come up with more empowering meanings to situations than the disempowering ones you started with.

Question 5: What do I honestly need to feel good about this situation?

Here you've decided you're going to have a positive emotion, so you might need more information. You've likely already realized with Question 3 that you don't have the full story. To feel good, you might need to change your perception. Or you might need to hear an apology from them. Conversely, you might need to apologize to them for making up some horrible meaning that isn't even true.

This releases you from your attachment to your reaction. Instead, you're making a conscious decision to experience a positive emotion and be in a positive state, and you're actively seeking what that would require.

Question 6: How would I go back to this person and get my needs met?

Within that question is also the decision to make sure the other person doesn't walk away feeling beat up, angry, or frustrated.

Now it's about the pursuit of win/win. Can we communicate with that outcome in mind? Sure we can. You can go to that person and make what we call a quality request. The way we teach it at Fortune is to start with the ultimate verbal softener. You begin by saying, "Hey, I need your help."

Because you are seeking a win/win, you must speak from your intention. That requires you to use the right tonality and the right physiology. The mindset that will help you is what we talked about earlier in this book: every response from another human being is either a loving response or a cry for help. If someone has hurt you, try looking at it as a cry for help masked as something else. This will lead you to more effective communication because you're drilling down into their reality.

This quality request you're going to make is actually a loving response. Approach it that way, and you'll marvel at the result.

Here's a simple example of a quality request: "Hey, I really need your help. When you didn't show up for our lunch appointment yesterday, I misinterpreted it. I put a wrong meaning to it, that you didn't care about our relationship. And I know that's not true. Why? Because I know who you are."

What most people do when they overreact is they make it an ad hominem attack, meaning they attack the person or their character rather than addressing the action itself, like the driver who may have been in a terrible hurry, but you labeled him a jerk. It's wrong and, as you know, not very helpful. You're going to reverse that.

With a quality request, you're not even challenging their intent. You may very well be trying to correct their behavior because people need to be called on their bullshit, and they need to know the impact of their actions and reactions. You are aiming for that result. The outcome is not to punish or release your hurt onto them but to understand and change behavior.

So you continue, saying, "I know who you are. So what I really need is some clarity. Can you give me some meaning I can assign to this that will make me feel better?"

This is not necessarily going to resolve the issue. But it puts it on a healthier path.

You may learn enough about that person to realize the relationship is important enough for them to change or for both of you to change.

You've given a loving response. And now you've vastly increased the odds of a loving response from them.

INTERPRETING LIFE EVENTS

I want you to take this concept of choosing your meaning beyond just personal interactions. Your interpretation of events has a profound effect on your state of mind and the quality of your life. Your ability to change the negative meaning of something to a more positive one is a sign of emotional fitness and mental toughness.

If you wake up tomorrow morning and your bank account shows zero, what meaning are you going to assign to that? Will you say, "I'm a failure?" Or will you see it as a wake-up call? Will you remind yourself the past doesn't equal the future? All it has to mean is the alarm clock just went off and you've got to get busy.

When I lost a million dollars at a very young age, I didn't believe it was an accident. I knew I had two choices. One choice was to throw a pity party for myself and to let it take me down and define me. The other choice was to say, "Hey, what do I need to do to get out of this? What is the meaning I need to assign here so I can rise from this?"

I could have ascribed the meaning that I was a failure. Instead, the meaning I chose was that there was something to learn here, and I had to figure out what it was. I had to believe there was a master plan and this was an awareness test.

Put in a spiritual way, I trusted God had a plan for me, but he wasn't going to execute it for me. It's not about avoiding pain. That's impossible. It's about finding your higher self. That's what the loss did for me. It put me on the path to my purpose. I've applied that belief and always work to find the positive in everything.

I believe in life there are no accidents, and everything happens for a reason. This may sound like I'm getting into my spiritual beliefs, and to a certain degree, I am. But my spiritual beliefs have evolved based on experience. I believe the universe will turn up the volume on me and increase my pain until I listen because that has happened to me over and over again. I believe people are essentially good if you give them a chance because that has been my experience. I believe when you give, it comes back to you tenfold because for me, it has. These experiences define my spirituality.

In the same way, I've come to believe in the power of choosing better meanings because of the profound impact it's had on my life. I make the effort to ask that very powerful question in every crisis, "What's great about this?"

By asking that question, you are operating from the assumption there is *always* a reason something happened, and you need to seek the good in it.

Of course, this is easy to do when something good is happening. It's easy to ascribe a positive meaning to a positive occurrence. (Even though sometimes pessimists don't!) But the life skill is doing it when things go bad, sometimes in a very serious way.

Shift from urge to intention.

I see this happen when a person loses someone close to them, especially when it's sudden. They ask, "Why would God take this person from me?" And certainly, there is going to be sadness and grief with the loss. But when it turns into a belief about a cruel God or a pointless universe, the meaning is doing more damage than the grief itself.

This is a time when it's hardest to ask what's great about the situation but it's when it's most important. You recall when I talked about losing my best friend to cancer. I grieved heavily for him. But I also knew he would have wanted me to extract something positive from his death. So I drew upon my positive energy, acknowledging I felt pain because I had lost a friend I loved so much. I knew that his message for me was to never leave anything on the table and to live to the fullest because I don't know how much time I have either.

Instead of blaming God, I chose to be grateful for the precious gift our friendship was and to learn a powerful lesson at the same time.

Everyone we know is going to die someday. It will hurt, and the grief may seem overwhelming. Understand that choosing your meaning doesn't mean you dismiss or ignore the gravity of the event. It means you look for the good in the hardship and allow yourself to experience that emotion, maybe alongside the other painful emotion. Find what positive meaning you can.

Another example would be the horrible events of September 11, 2001. This was a tremendous tragedy, where 2,996 people lost their lives. I am in no way diminishing that loss, especially for their families. But let's reflect on all the good that came from it.

It awakened an awareness that something deeply troubling was occurring in the Middle East and the hatred towards America was intensifying. It couldn't be ignored.

We were inspired by the heroism of the passengers on United Airlines Flight 93.

We came to revere our firefighters and police officers and their courage and dedication.

We became aware of how much more had to be done to increase airline safety.

Best of all, the whole country pulled together to the greatest degree since WWII.

The pandemic of 2020 also had a profound effect on people. It was not all negative. People started spending more time with their families. Businesses realized they had to pivot to survive and that no future was so certain it couldn't be disrupted in a day. We developed a much faster system to create vaccines that will eventually save millions of lives. And the list goes on.

If you asked 100 successful people what got them where they are today, I guarantee you every one of them would say they found the positive value in every crisis, every loss, and every setback in their lives.

Nothing is all bad or all good. But if you want to live an empowered life, you have to understand that nothing in life has meaning except the meaning we give to it. Then you can start choosing those meanings, one by one, and creating a joyful, positive, fulfilling life.

POWERFUL QUESTIONS:

- What crisis in my past can I ascribe a powerful, positive meaning to?

- When do I choose to react before I have sufficient information to justify my reaction?

- Am I skilled at making quality requests?

- What's great about this?

- What else can this mean?

32

FOUR ARCHETYPES AND THE EGO

IF I COULD POINT TO ONE PERSON IN MY LIFE WHO HAD THE most impact on me, it would be Dr. Wayne Dyer. He is often recognized as one of the first great teachers of peak performance and personal development. And he was a great motivational speaker with a valuable message. But as time went on, he moved beyond that message to a spiritual one.

After years of lecturing and writing books on personal growth, he made a shift. And he attributed that to an understanding of the four archetypes of a human being. This was derived from the teachings of Carl Jung, but Wayne put his own spin on it and applied it to his own life and teaching.

Wayne helped me understand the ego is the worst part of us. It's the part of us that has a need to be right. It's the part of us that lives in scarcity and believes in a zero-sum game. The part that wants to go to war rather than seek peace.

Ego forces you to live in a reactive state and not see choices. And ultimately, Wayne points out, the ego separates you from your spirit. You lose connection to your spiritual self as well as your spiritual connection to everyone else.

THE FOUR ARCHETYPES

The four archetypes are a progression of transformational stages from birth to death. I will break down each of the archetypes and show how they are intertwined with the development and control of the ego.

The Athlete

When we are born into this world, we begin as the archetype of the Athlete. This first stage is parallel to what any athlete does. You spend most of your time strengthening, growing, training, learning, getting better, and working on constant and never-ending improvement. This doesn't necessarily mean you are in an athletic pursuit at this stage. But you are learning to walk, talk, read and interact with society, and you're certainly developing physical skills but also skills in general. Your parents guide you through this stage, as does the educational system. But this is all in preparation for the second stage.

The Warrior

As the Warrior, you go out into the world with all you've learned and lay claim to what will be yours. You will be competitive, aggressive, and determined, all while refining the skills you've learned by testing them on the battlefield of life. We all need to do this. This is your pursuit of a career, mate, reputation, and position in society. This is the beginning of finding your fortune.

The challenge with the Warrior archetype is that even though you are making gains in life because of your competitive spirit and applying your skills, the ego really drives the Warrior mentality. This was where I was in my twenties: aggressively pursuing businesses, staking my claim in the world, driven by my ego.

The Statesman

Then there is the next stage, the third archetype, which is the Statesman (I want to use the word Wayne taught, so try to think of this in a gender-neutral way). This is one of the greatest shifts you can make in your life because now you start seeing things differently. Your mentality shifts outside yourself, and you reverse many of the mindsets of the Warrior.

Much of what I've laid out in the previous chapters is elements of living in the third archetype. You let go of the scarcity mindset and see the world as abundant. You pursue win/win. You lead with your giving hand, and you start to realize—and even feel—that we are all connected as human beings. You are releasing yourself from the control of the ego, and it's a very satisfying place to be.

It still requires work, just as the Warrior archetype did, but from an entirely different mindset and with different motives and purpose. The reward is about connection, not conquering, and comes from giving instead of gaining.

When I teach this in seminars, I am quick to point out these archetypes are not an automatic chronological progression. Far from it. You don't naturally progress from Athlete to Warrior at eighteen years old and then to Statesman at fifty-five. Some people don't go into Warrior mode until they're thirty or older. And many never progress beyond that.

I know people in their eighties who are still operating in the Warrior archetype, competing, playing a zero-sum game, driven by their ego. And they will die that way. Many people believe that's all there is. What a waste, I say.

Nothing guarantees that you will move to the Statesman archetype. It's a conscious choice. If you're lucky, you will take the time and ask, "Is this enough?" And you will be able to look at your Warrior life and say, "There must be more. There must be some greater satisfaction somehow."

And then that shift can begin. Hopefully every part of this book shows you how you can become a statesperson. You move from self-centered to other-centered, and your world opens up to a whole new level of joy and satisfaction that the Warrior didn't believe was possible.

Archetype of the Spirit

There is still one more level, the fourth archetype. Wayne called it the Archetype of the Spirit. I would define it specifically as a shift upward to seeing your life's role as inspiration.

At this level, you have moved completely outside yourself. Your life is dedicated to making the world a better place, with little or no thought for yourself. I don't believe everyone needs to reach this level or that we are all destined to do so, but it helps to understand that it's possible and to understand people who've reached that level.

The greatest shift occurs when you move from self-centered to other-centered.

We know some of their names. Mahatma Gandhi. Nelson Mandela. Their power to inspire is so strong it still resonates with thousands and even millions of people, motivating them to be better simply by the example of these leaders.

One of the best examples I can give you is Mother Theresa. I heard a story about her that occurred while she was on a book tour, going around to different radio stations in the US. She went to a station in Phoenix, Arizona, and later, the people working there said that from the moment she walked into the building, they could feel her presence. That's how powerful she was. It was as if she raised the consciousness of the whole building without a word, simply by being there.

The radio host began to interview her and heaped praise on her for all her achievements. She stopped him at a certain point and thanked him but then explained that she wasn't there to talk about herself. She said, "I'm here to talk about the homeless people who are sleeping on the streets in Phoenix. I'm here to talk about what we can do to make the world a better place. I'm here to raise our consciousness level so we care about all people as if we are all one. Because we are."

That was how she approached her whole life, which may be beyond your imagination for yourself right now. The question for you here is, what archetype are you currently in? You might still be young, the Athlete, training for your future. More likely you are in Warrior mode, straddling the gap to Statesman. Knowing what you know now, how quickly can you make a shift in your life beyond Warrior to Statesman?

The recipe is simple. Release yourself from the ego.

Also, you don't have to be Mother Theresa to decide to move to Inspiration. You are never too young to make the world a better place. Writing this book is about me working my way up to that fourth archetype. I'm not doing this for myself. This is not ego driven. I hope you can sense that. I'm doing this to pay it forward. If I can change one person's life, save a life, or make someone believe the past is not their future, then this book has been worthwhile. And that's inspiration.

I'll end with my favorite teaching from Wayne Dyer about the path to this fourth archetype. He shared Chardin's famous quote: "You are not a human being having a spiritual experience. You're a spiritual being having a human experience."

Words to live by.

POWERFUL QUESTIONS:

- What archetype am I currently living?

- Am I willing to release my ego?

- Do I believe we are all connected?

33

WHO MADE YOU?

This chapter is going to be a little different because there's an exercise included. The inspiration for it was a scene from the movie *A Beautiful Day in the Neighborhood,* starring Tom Hanks as Mister Rogers. At one point in the movie, Rogers asks a reporter who's been interviewing him, "Tell me, who made you?"

The point of his question was that every one of us has been shaped by other people in our lives. They were the people who influenced us, gave us our worldview, or made us feel like we could accomplish something. It may have been someone who was a steady part of our life—a teacher we had one year or a crazy uncle we admired.

We are an accumulation of all the people we've crossed paths with in our lives. Some had a strong influence on us and others very little. The idea in this chapter is for you to reflect on who those people were.

For me, it was, of course, my parents. And my grandmother, whom I mentioned. But it was also my wife. We married young, and her enduring love and patience shaped me into a much better man than I would have become if left to my own devices.

And then there were people I met as a teenager who taught me little things while I was working at the gas station. I held them in high esteem and modeled my behavior after them.

We are an accumulation of all the people who influenced us in our lives.

Later it was Wayne Dyer, who I was fortunate enough to meet and spend time with. Dr. Gary Mcleod had a huge influence on me when I came into the dental field. Tony Robbins believed in me and trusted me, and that created a turning point. I can name several more people along the way, and it is still happening. I meet someone, and they have an impact on me. And I sincerely hope I have been an impactful person for some people in my life.

But this is about you. I want you to reflect on your past and make a list of the people who shaped you. Really take your time with this. Sit quietly, and plan to spend an hour or more uninterrupted. Think about the person you are today and why you are the way you are. And with the name of each person, list the lessons that came from them.

It may be something good they did, hopefully, but sometimes it's something that didn't seem so good at the time. For example, I have friends who had alcoholic fathers, and because of it, they barely touch a drink. Think about everyone who made a strong impression on you. Who made you believe in yourself, or saw something in you that you didn't?

As always, family members will be on your list. But here are some other suggestions to spark your memory:

- A high school teacher or college professor

- An older sibling

- A scoutmaster

- Your priest, or rabbi, or mullah

- A guidance counselor

- Your first boss

- Your college roommate

- Your athletic coach

- Your first love

- Your second love

- A mentor

- A professional colleague

- A person you met on a plane who gave you a career idea

- Your AA sponsor

- A famous person who took the time to talk to you

I think you could probably come up with twenty people or more. And be sure to include the details of how they affected you and how they contributed to who you are today.

Reflect on these names, and be grateful for each one of these people.

And here's one more important step. For any of them who are still alive, take some time and write them a letter, or give them and call and let them know their contribution to your life. Maybe you haven't talked to this person in twenty years. Imagine if you told them, out of the blue, something like this: "I just wanted to let you know that you are still a part of who I am. And you are one of the reasons I am where I am today. Thank you so much. I'm so grateful for you. And I just wanted to tell you the impact you had on me. I haven't ever forgotten it."

Imagine how that would make them feel. Imagine how it would make you feel.

POWERFUL QUESTIONS:

- Who had the most impact on my life?

- Who believed in me?

- Who knocked me out of my rut?

- Who called me on my bullshit?

- Who loved me unconditionally?

34

CHOOSE YOUR ENVIRONMENT

To succeed, you need to choose your environment. This primarily means choosing the people you associate with, but also places—meetings, classes, clubs, sports, hobbies—should be growth-oriented and aligned with your values.

There are few things more important than who you surround yourself with. Your growth journey is either supported and inspired by your peers, or they slow you down, drag you down, or even derail you.

You will find there are people and environments where you are encouraged to grow, where new ideas appear, and you refine your goals based on these places and peers. When you reflect on who made you in the previous chapter, think about the people who gave you the boost you needed in life. Those are the kind of people you need to surround yourself with.

THE JACUZZI EFFECT

As human beings, we tend to adapt to the behaviors of our peers. We always want to fit in. What happens invariably when we decide to find our fortune is that some of the people we surrounded ourselves with when we were younger are uncomfortable with our evolution. They won't like who we are becoming because they sense we are leaving them behind.

If you change, that makes them uncomfortable. If you become ambitious, they don't like how it reflects on their lack of ambition. And it goes deeper than that. Most of those people live in scarcity, so if you decide to embrace an abundance mindset, they will not support it. They will be critical of it. They may mock it, even.

I see this happen very often with people who come to my seminars, and they suddenly become inspired and motivated, perhaps for the first time in their lives. And what happens is what I call the Jacuzzi Effect. They spend a weekend with a whole group of people who are there to improve, who are energetic and positive, eager to set goals and achieve them. They get swept up in this positive energy, like a group of people all relaxing together in a jacuzzi, having the same wonderful experience.

And then they go home.

They try to explain all they've learned to their friends or their significant other, what they've decided to accomplish, and what they're going to change about themselves. And people look at them like they've got two heads. They'll hear things, like, "Right. That'll never happen," or "I see you drank the Kool-Aid." They encounter discouragement at every turn and gradually slip back into their old selves.

It breaks my heart when I see this happen. So I warn people to expect it. Then I say part of their life plan has to be to choose peers who will support and inspire them and seek environments to help them grow and create discoveries.

It doesn't mean these people in your life don't love you. They do. Some of them genuinely don't want you to get hurt by dreaming too big and failing. They are trapped in scarcity, so their honest emotion is to be protective of you.

Seek out empowering environments and let something hit you.

You are then faced with a hard choice. You might need to let that person go and not spend time with them. This is not my first recommendation because it is hard to do and almost feels unloving. What I suggest is you first call them out on their limiting belief. Ask them why they are so attached to that belief, and point out how detrimental it could be to their happiness. Let them know that you are not judging them or wanting to leave them behind.

If you are strong enough, you could become the person who inspires them and shakes them out of their disempowering beliefs and bad habits. But don't count on it. Everyone has an epiphany at their own pace. They may need to see you create a better life for yourself for years before they learn. And they may resent you the whole time.

Sometimes you just have to let that person go completely. It may even be a whole peer group. As is often the case, like-minded people hang out together. I remind people that if you lie down with dogs, you wake up with fleas. If your current peer group likes to go out drinking every night, does drugs on the weekends, hates their jobs and their bosses, and cheats on their spouses, I hope I don't have to explain this group will not support you in finding your fortune.

I understand you love these people. But the most loving thing you need to do may be for yourself. This is where emotional fitness and mental toughness come in. You are likely not going to be strong enough to break them out of their habits, and you're much more likely to slip back into them yourself. You must summon the fortitude to let some people go.

THE UPWARD SPIRAL

There is a great lesson taught in Alcoholics Anonymous, which is if you don't want to slip, don't go where it's slippery. This lesson applies to all of us and to many more situations than just going to a bar.

When peers challenge you for "becoming a different person," I would respond by saying, "No, I'm just learning how to take better care of myself. I hope you would want me to be happy. But we may find ourselves diametrically opposed in our thinking, and I have to be careful how I spend my time. I want something different, so I have to behave differently. And I need people around me who support that."

Then they can decide if they want to be one of those people. Please understand and accept that if you're growing, you will outgrow people. It's a fact of life.

If you're at this point, you need new friends. Better friends. And these new people who are aligned with your thinking will support you, encourage you, teach you, and believe in you. These people become your brothers- and sisters-in-arms in the pursuit of your dreams. Some of them you will inspire, and you can offer help and insight you've gained along the way. It's a fabulous upward spiral for everyone.

You will eventually get to the point where you seek out specific people you want to have in your peer group. You may be looking for a mentor, a colleague, or even a partner. It may be someone with complementary skills, someone smarter than you, or someone with much more experience. Or it could just be someone who is aligned with your thinking and your new mindset, so you want them around.

I do this all the time, and it always starts with alignment. The person doesn't have to agree with everything I say, but they have to lead with their giving hand and believe in win/win and abundance. It will always start there, with their core values.

Now, I'm not telling you to be a social climber. That's not the goal. You are looking for like-minded people to build relationships with so you can both contribute to each other.

I'm lucky. I still have great friends from my youth. We've always supported each other's paths. We don't drag each other down.

Hopefully you will have some people like this, too, who will always be in your life.

THE "BETTER" STRATEGY

You also need to put yourself in new environments and expose yourself to new ideas and new approaches. Get around where it's better, and let something hit you. It's about awareness, but it starts with being in a place where there is something to be aware of. Always push yourself out of your comfort zone, meet new people, and expose yourself to new ideas.

Getting to a better place stretches your goals. I always use the example of Roger Bannister, who was the first person to run a mile in under four minutes. As remarkable as that was, what was more amazing was that within a few months, three more people did it. When you get around where people are better, you believe more is possible.

In Fortune Management we do this for our clients. We create events and special groups where our members can meet peers from all around the country and discover new ways of doing things or new ways of thinking. Or they can just make new friends. It's exciting to see and be a part of it.

We have built a company consisting of people who share the same core values, and that makes us much stronger because everyone is growth-oriented and supports and raises each other up. If you can create that for yourself, you'll be unstoppable.

You must actively choose environments that empower you. You may even need to move to a new neighborhood or city. This is part of a life by design. And always be seeking peers who elevate you, resonate with you, and dream as big as you do.

POWERFUL QUESTIONS:

- Who are the peers who empower me?

- Are there people in my life I need to leave behind?

- Do I live, work, and play in environments that support my growth mindset?

- Who would I like to add to my peer group?

35

EMPATHY
AND KINDNESS

When it comes to finding your fortune and discovering the true riches of life, I have found empathy and kindness to be instrumental in that path.

Empathy is a life skill. Let me first make a clear distinction between empathy and sympathy. They are often considered the same, but to me they are almost polar opposites. Sympathy means you are feeling something *for* someone. You are expressing your own emotion or opinion. Empathy is feeling something *with* someone. With empathy, you identify with what the other person is feeling.

For example, a friend has just told you she lost her job. You could say, "I'm so sorry you lost your job. Your boss is a jerk." That's sympathy. You're expressing your feeling and viewpoint.

An empathetic response would be, "That sucks. You must be feeling pretty dejected right now. Let's go for coffee together."

With empathy, you put yourself in the other person's shoes and try to understand what they are feeling. You're not searching for your own reaction.

As I said, empathy is a life skill. It's not natural. It's a release of the ego to feel empathy. And as such, it is also a move away from being in the Warrior archetype and toward the Statesman. Remember, the Statesman has moved outside of themselves and released their ego so they can focus on others.

FEEL, FELT, FOUND

We have something we teach our clients at Fortune Management. It's a way to communicate with patients who are feeling apprehensive about the cost and discomfort of treatments. It's a communication template you can use in most situations when people are having an emotional reaction and you are trying to influence them.

It uses these three words: feel, felt, and found.

Here is an example. A patient has been told they need $5,000 in periodontal treatment. This is a complete surprise to the patient, and bad news. The patient has some sticker shock and also some dread about the pain of the treatment. In other words, he has an emotional reaction. What most people and most doctors do when faced with a person reacting emotionally is they make the mistake of going the rational route. They try to explain with facts and figures why the person shouldn't feel the way they do.

That doesn't honor the person's emotions, and it's also completely ineffective. Instead, use *feel, felt, found*. Like this.

"I understand how you *feel*, Alex. I've had many patients who've *felt* the same way. But they *found* we were able to work through the financial difficulties with them. Also, after it was done, they *found* they were much happier with the health of their gums and smile."

You first acknowledged their emotion, and then you validated it. And then you laid out a new emotional pathway for them by telling them how other people felt. You didn't default to logic because they weren't having a logical reaction. They were having an emotional reaction.

How often in your life do you make this mistake, trying to solve an emotional issue with logic and reason? Does it work? This is why you need to learn true empathy. Then you are meeting the person where they are.

Empathy is one of the highest forms of kindness. When you come from a place of kindness, making that choice whenever possible, suddenly you're able to be empathetic. Again, this is movement toward the Statesman level of life.

KINDNESS

If you recall, I talked about priming myself every morning with the four emotions I always want to come from: gratitude, happiness, abundance, and kindness. I've learned over time you can always come from a place of kindness. It becomes a filter that always leads you to a loving choice.

When you believe every human response is either a cry for help or a loving expression, then kindness is your pathway to always choose to meet that cry for help with a loving response of your own. Empathy is a loving response. Kindness is the intention that opens your heart to do it.

Empathy doesn't necessarily mean you have experienced the same thing the other person has. It means you put yourself in their place. That's all you have to do. If someone has lost their child in an accident, you don't have to have lost a child yourself to be empathetic. You just have to ask yourself how you would feel if that happened to you.

Empathy is fueled by kindness.

It's a lot easier to be sympathetic. Then you don't really have to feel anything difficult. Empathy is hard sometimes, but that's why it's so effective. It's coming from knowledge as a Statesman that we are all connected in some way and then determining the kindest thing you can do.

Kindness and empathy will affect every aspect of your career and relationships. You will be a better salesperson, a better leader, a better spouse, and a better friend.

I'll give you an example of this in business. Danny Myer, the founder of Shake Shack, the burger chain that started as a single storefront in Madison Square Park in New York City and now has over 6,000 employees, has a simple guideline for hiring.

He assesses each employee on their EQ, or emotional intelligence. This counts for more than half of the reason to hire the person or not. He measures it on six parameters, and within those are two key ones you might guess: empathy and kindness. Naturally, Meyer wants employees to be able to learn the skills to do the job, but it's equally important they know how to interact with people in a positive way. They need to make the customer feel valued, appreciated, and important.

To me, this is brilliant, and the proof is in the success of Shake Shack. It went from being a single hot dog stand in 2001 to 264 locations worldwide, with a market value of almost $5 billion. Yep, that's billion. If it can work for a fast-food business, it can work for you.

The choice of kindness and the skill of empathy will serve you all your days. Develop them, and no matter what financial wealth you may achieve, your life will always be rich.

POWERFUL QUESTIONS:

- When do I find myself not choosing kindness?

- Do I respond with empathy or with logic and reason when faced with an emotional reaction?

- Do I value the EQ of those around me and those who work for me?

.

36

OWN IT

I BELIEVE THAT EVERY SINGLE THING THAT HAPPENS TO ME IN my life, I am responsible for. Break that word down: "response" and "able." I always have an ability to respond simply because I am alive. This is when it becomes about choice. You have to make a decision, and it's a big one. Are you going to live a proactive life? Or are you going to live in reactivity? If you choose to be a proactive human being, it means you have to adopt a string of two-letter words. They are: *If it's going to be, it's up to me.*

It's about being responsible for your own life. It's about owning it. This is also an abundant belief. The scarcity mindset says, "It's not my fault. I'm not in control. Shit happens, and it always happens to me. I can only react to what happens. I didn't have a choice."

The reactive person chooses denial or excuses or gets defensive and abdicates as much responsibility as possible. The scarcity mindset is on a constant quest to assign blame.

In this chapter, I invite you to send blame out of your life. Eliminate it forever as a response choice. Take responsibility for everything in your life. The day you decide to do that, your life truly begins.

TAKING CONTROL

How many people around you choose blame as their default reaction? They blame the political party in charge, their boss, their husband or wife, the economy, the capitalists, the socialists, the immigrants, or the wealthy. They blame COVID-19. Look at the absurdity of that. They are so determined to not take responsibility for anything they will blame a microscopic organism rather than own anything.

No matter what happens, you can always find someone else to blame. But for me that would be the scariest place to be because it means you have no control over the direction of your life. Every outcome is now beyond your grasp. Every solution has to come from somewhere else.

Think about it. If you don't have any control over your situation, how the hell are you going to fix it? When you reverse that mindset and take ownership of every aspect of your life, it becomes an empowering belief. It means you can change it. In fact, it's up to you to change it. And that's a whole lot better than hoping somebody cares about you enough to solve it for you.

This is the trap of entitlement. When you believe someone else is responsible for solving your problems, it means you are beholden to them and living on their timetable. There are people who have been waiting an entire lifetime for someone else to fix their problems.

You may say, "Bernie, some things really aren't my responsibility. I didn't make a tornado rip through my house." But that's just a dodge. Of course, things will happen, and some of them will be terrible. What you own is what you do about what happened. What you own is your response, which is in your control. You chose to live in Oklahoma. You chose to save money and not build a tornado shelter. And now you're sitting in a tent waiting for FEMA to build you another house. Own your part in what happened, and then do something.

When you accept responsibility for everything in your life, your life truly begins.

Stuff happens. You get a tax audit. Own the fact you hired a lousy accountant. The stock market took a nosedive. You chose to not diversify your portfolio. Now choose what you're going to do about it.

When I lost all that money in the restaurant business, I had chosen to ignore the high risks in that industry. So I owned the consequences. I could have found blame everywhere: my chef, my manager, the location. But I was at the center of it all.

I rejoice in that whole catastrophe because I had the understanding that it was up to me to fix it. And that wasn't discouraging. It was powerful because I didn't have to wait for anything or anyone. FEMA wasn't coming. I just had to step up.

When you own it, you realize that powerful truth from Jim Rohn, that if you want your life to get better, you have to get better. To me, that beats the hell out of sitting around waiting for a stimulus check, a bailout, or a lawyer to get me a settlement to live on.

BE PROACTIVE

When you accept responsibility, you can focus on adding value, getting creative, and evolving. That's a life by design, not by divine intervention.

On the other hand, look at how much people spend on lottery tickets every day. Billions. They expect fate or random chance to change their lives. To me, few things say, "I'm not in control of the direction of my life," like someone buying lottery tickets.

I get the appeal of blaming someone else. It's not fun to take responsibility for the bad stuff you've created. It's not fun to do the hard stuff on the path to achievement, but emotional fitness and mental toughness will you get there. And you develop those by owning it, by accepting responsibility.

I'll even accept responsibility for things I am pretty sure I didn't cause. Why? Because it puts me in solution mode. I don't burn a single calorie on the blame game. I go straight to proactive mode.

I even help people to take responsibility when I am being empathetic. I've learned to put a positive spin on my empathy. For example, I may have a client tell me they just got divorced. And I say, gently, "Well, congratulations."

They look at me and say, "What do you mean?"

And I respond by telling them, "I understand this feels hard right now. But I also understand how miserable you were in that marriage and how miserable your spouse was too. So I'm congratulating you because now you can open yourself up to the love you deserve. That time is here. Embrace the pain. Congratulations."

It's a subtle way of saying, "Own it." Don't blame your ex. Don't blame how hard you had to work so you couldn't pay enough attention to her. Take responsibility, and change the course of your life from here. The past does not equal the future. You create it.

Of course, I am empathetic, so I may not say that to the client all in one conversation, but my goal with everyone is to help them see how they can own the path of their life simply by a decision to do so.

Finally, back when I told you to touch it once and said, "I don't own anything," you know very well that had a different meaning. Don't try to trip me up. I delegate vigorously, but I take responsibility for everything in my life. I recommend you do too.

POWERFUL QUESTIONS:

- When do I react by blaming someone or something besides myself?

- What do I think I am entitled to?

- How am I responsible?

37

LAW OF ATTRACTION

You will hear a lot spoken about the law of attraction. I have a unique interpretation of it based on my own life experiences.

There was a book and a video that came out several years ago called *The Secret,* which presented a theory of the law of attraction, and I personally think that book did as much damage as it did good.

The confusion comes when people translate goal-setting, which, as you know, I believe is important, into a process of making requests from the universe.

Goals are meant to stretch you, challenge you, and force you to make a plan of action to achieve them. Goals help you dig down to your passion and purpose. But if you are told all you need to do is ask the universe for what you want and then sit back and wait, you will be sorely disappointed.

This interpretation of the law of attraction puts out the concept that the universe is a mail order catalog. You want a bigger house? Ask the universe. You want a promotion, ask the universe. Make a vision board. Make a list of what you want, and sit back and relax. This makes it seem like the universe is just an all-powerful Santa Claus.

Sometimes people believe you don't just request. You demand. It's the force of your demand that will manifest your goals and wishes. That's nonsense.

I hope you've found that this has not been my message. This doesn't conform at all to "If it's going to be, it's up to me." It's the opposite. It's making the universe responsible.

I see people get trapped in what I call "request mode." I see this as just one notch below blame mode. Where is the personal responsibility? Where is the growth, the striving, the learning? This is what life is truly about.

To me, this is not the law of attraction. My law of attraction, as you can imagine, is based on action. Just like everything else in this book and in life, it comes down to the quality of the questions you're asking.

Asking for what you want, what you need, or what you think you deserve is not a high-quality request. What if you changed the request? What if the new questions were, "How can I give? How can I serve?"

This new understanding is what changed my life thirty years ago. It also helped me to get out of Warrior mode and become a States-man, doing the life skills work I've done with Fortune.

SERVICE IS THE KEY

Here's what I discovered that changed everything for me. The universe is just a mirror image of us. That's all it is. If you spend your whole life setting goals that are really just requests of what you need and want, you are operating in request mode, and the universe will reflect that. If you are making your list of the cars, mates, and success you want, the universe hears, "Gimme, gimme, gimme!"

That's what will be reflected back to you. The universe will suck the life out of you because you are in "take mode." So the universe takes. It takes your motivation, your drive, and your willpower until it's gone. You're looking around, depleted, saying, "Where's all my stuff?"

This is the universe saying you've got it wrong. This is the universe laughing at you.

Here's the magic. The minute you get out of request mode and start asking, "How can I serve?" the whole world opens up in infinite abundance, because the universe heard that. It's not laughing at you. It's smiling and saying, "What can I do for you?" And it will flow to you from unexpected directions.

However, it's not about keeping score. It's not about tricking the universe by saying, "I'm going to ask how I can give so I can get a lot more in return." It doesn't work that way. The joy and satisfaction come from serving. The true wealth and abundant riches are in the moments you are giving and serving. The universe supports you in these efforts, widening your ability to impact and influence.

This is the real law of attraction: you attract who you are and what you give, not what you want or demand. I learned this by transforming my life to one of service and leading with my giving hand.

Because of this, I have been rewarded tenfold, but also seldom in kind. Many times you won't receive in the same areas where you gave or in the same amounts you gave. You'll serve people in your life who will never be able to thank you or pay you back.

You attract who you are, not what you want.

During the times when people do thank me, my response is, "If you want to thank me, do well. Make a difference. Make me proud of you." If someone takes the knowledge or insight I've given them, runs with it, and makes it a better world even in a small way, then I have been rewarded.

I have been blessed with an abundant life, many times from completely different and unexpected places. It has sometimes been financial, but I've also been rewarded with relationships, unique shared experiences, or lessons for myself that make life better for me and everyone in my circle of influence.

I am grateful for every opportunity I am given to serve, whether it is for an individual or a group of people. I invite you to believe in the universe and what it can do for you. It's waiting to reflect the best you can offer.

POWERFUL QUESTIONS:

- Have I backed up my goals with action?

- How can I serve?

- Do I understand the mirror effect of the universe?

38

LIFE MASTERY

Every principle I've offered here contributes to the concept of life mastery. I hope you realize by this point I don't just mean the aggregation of wealth. True life mastery doesn't just equate to a certain income level. It means you have mastered every element of the life wheel and found richness everywhere in many forms.

The good news is that if you focus on continually expanding and tapping into your full potential in these six areas of your life, you're going to be better than fine; you're going to be great. You're going to master life. The bad news for most people is that they don't focus on all six. You can't neglect any of them.

Let's remember what those six are.

SIX AREAS OF MASTERY

1. **Emotional Mastery:** You need emotional fitness and mental toughness to be a good leader, rise to meet

challenges, and deal with losses in your personal and professional life. You need to manage your state and know when to celebrate. You need to choose the emotions you operate from every day. You've learned to embrace the pain and life's lessons. And you will take a stand when it counts.

2. **Physical Mastery:** You need to take care of your body for the long term, which means what you do every day matters. What you eat, how much you sleep, and how consistently you exercise are all essential. You need goals and an action plan. You need to understand that appearance matters, and you need to get around like-minded people who also believe in physical fitness.

3. **Relationship Mastery:** Some of the greatest riches in your life will be your family and friends. If you are blessed with children, you want to be the best parent you can be. And with your life partner, most of all, you want that relationship to be deep, enduring, and filled with joy. You have to choose your meanings so your response always comes from a loving place. You must endeavor to always make it a win/win for everyone involved, especially the people you love. You need humor and a smile, and you must come from abundance and believe that people are basically good. And you are always evolving.

4. **Career Mastery:** You need to be determined to be the best and offer the best you possibly can in your chosen profession. You need to refine your influence skills and deliver win/wins. You will merge work and play,

find your passion, harness your energy, and tap into your hunger. You'll do your homework. You've built a personal brand, and you cherish the brand of your company. You embrace technology and work and speak from intention. And you've refined the art of touching it once. You embrace the pain and use it to grow and learn. Most of all, you need to learn to serve and to approach all situations leading with your giving hand.

5. **Financial Mastery:** This one is critical. You need to understand your relationship with money, how money works, and how to protect it. This means you appreciate business, do your homework, and set goals. You also see how the law of attraction works and put yourself in better places that reinforce your belief in abundance. You understand it's okay to do well by doing good. You are keenly aware that having money makes it possible for you to give more, serve more, and contribute more. And without money, you will always be struggling.

6. **Spiritual Mastery:** To keep your ego in check, you need to believe in a higher power. I don't think it matters what you call it as long as you see the connection between yourself and everyone else in the world. You need faith to get you through the tough times. Generosity and gratitude are integral to your spiritual life. Empathy and kindness must pour from you in all interactions. You understand there are no accidents and that your ego is often the enemy. Empathy and kindness drive your personal fulfillment as much as any financial gain.

I hope you can see how all the elements of the life wheel build on each other. To achieve Relationship Mastery, you will need Emotional Mastery and Spiritual Mastery. Maintaining your health to achieve Physical Mastery will often require money and time, so you'd better have Financial Mastery and Career Mastery. They are all interlocked, just as the principles I've laid out for you affect several elements of life mastery.

You can't neglect any of the six elements of the life wheel. They are interdependent. They reinforce each other. And if one is deficient, the quality of your life is seriously diminished.

THE PATH TO MASTERY

The executive who's achieved massive success but sacrificed their health and relationship with their family has not mastered life. They only focused on two elements and neglected the others.

The person who says family is all that matters and neglects their career and financial mastery finds they can't provide for their family or give their kids the education they would like.

This well-rounded approach to life mastery is what we teach our clients at Fortune Management. I start every day by focusing on my life wheel to remind myself of what is important and what a truly balanced life looks like.

I also am keenly aware that none of us is perfect. At thirty, I was all about making money. I had great friendships but didn't have emotional fitness. I gave in to anger easily. I had abandoned the faith of my upbringing and not replaced it with any other spiritual beliefs. I had no balance. But I learned these principles that I'm offering to you, sometimes painfully. I changed, and life got better.

We all make mistakes, and we all wander off our path. We are all learning. You will not reach a perfect ten in any one of these areas of your life. But if you apply *kaizen* to each one, constantly seeking to improve in all six areas, you will achieve mastery. Along with that, you'll achieve fulfillment.

I truly believe we were born into this life with everything we need. We don't need outside forces to have an incredible life. It is all within us if we are aware, generous of heart, and open to change.

Mastery is a journey. The journey itself is where the joy and satisfaction come from. This is a recipe for living your life to the fullest. It worked for me, and I know it can work for you.

39

MAHALO

WHEN PEOPLE TO TRAVEL TO HAWAII, THEY OFTEN LEARN to say *mahalo* as a way of saying thank you in the native tongue. But it means something more in the true Polynesian dialect.

Many years ago, when the Hawaiian chieftains gathered together, they greeted each other by holding the other man's face and saying, "Mahalo," as they breathed into the man's mouth, with the "ha" being the breath. It was meant as gift of breath and therefore life, so it had a deep spiritual meaning.

For most of my life, Hawaii has been a special place for me. On my list of "who made me," I would actually include the beautiful state and people of Hawaii. It is a group of islands with thirteen different microclimates, from volcanos to tropical rainforests. And Hawaiians are some of the most wonderful and giving people in the world.

I started going to Hawaii in my teens and years later bought a home in Maui. My family and I spent many months there each year. When I sold that home, it left a hole in my heart. I had a longing for those islands that couldn't be replaced.

Years later, I began to meet dentists who flew to the mainland to take continuing education courses. They told me there was no service offering this type of training in Hawaii. So I made the decision to launch a Fortune franchise there. Now it has been over twenty years, and I am blessed with not just many clients but wonderful friends, and I get to go back there all the time. The word for family in Hawaiian is *ohana*. The people there are my Hawaii ohana.

Back to the deeper meaning of mahalo. While it is used as "Thank you" by tourists, in Hawaiian it means, "With ultimate respect and gratitude."

What a beautiful word. I end most of my email communications with that word, and I end every presentation with an explanation of the word's deeper meaning. I give my audience a final "mahalo" for giving me their time and attention.

And so to you, dear reader, my hope is that I have inspired you in some way and moved you on your path to finding your own fortune. And for your time and attention, I say, *Mahalo.*

ACKNOWLEDGMENTS

I have many mahalos to those who made me.

Wayne Dyer, who taught me how to make the shift from Warrior to Statesman.

Jim Rohn, who taught me that if life was going to get better, I needed to get better.

Tony Robbins, who taught me to awaken the giant within me.

Nancy Stoltz, for completing me and teaching me how to be a better person.

Gary McLeod, for trusting me with his powerful vision of Fortune Management.

Mom and Dad, for their unconditional love.

My grandmother, for her grace.

Jennifer and Michael, for giving me a master motive to succeed.

The men and women of Fortune Management, who all strive to make the world a better place.

Dentistry, for helping me to understand what truly purposeful work can be.

Fred Joyal, for putting all my thoughts into words, as only Fred can.

APPENDIX

COMPANIES I AM
CURRENTLY INVOLVED WITH:

Fortune Management

Fortune Management is a nationwide executive coaching organization for healthcare practices. It has been operating since 1989, and is the largest dental coaching business in the country. It teaches best practices, optimal systems, leadership skills and managerial excellence to practitioners at every level of success. Bernie has served as Chairman of the Board and Chief Executive Officer for twenty years.

Northeast Sequoia Private Client Group

Northeast Sequoia is a boutique financial advising and investment strategy company. It manages over $1 billion in assets for its clients, offering bespoke investment solutions with a mind to the security and long-term safety of its clients' assets, with a focus on creating multi-generational wealth. It's CEO of thirty-six years, Mark Murphy, was recognized as one of the top 500 financial advisors by *Forbes* magazine for 2021. Bernie is a shareholder and board member.

OraCare

OraCare is a unique and highly effective oral rinse distributed solely through dental practices. It is an ideal solution for periodontal issues as well as dry mouth and bad breath. Bernie is a founding investor and partner in OraCare.

TruBlu

TruBlu is a dental services platform offering an ever-expanding range of solutions to independent, technology-minded dentists. It focuses on leveling the playing field for independent dentists and preserving private practice dentistry in the United States. Bernie is a founding member and serves as Chairman of the Board.

RECOMMENDED READING

BOOKS THAT PUT ME
ON THE PATH:

Think and Grow Rich by Napoleon Hill

Change Your Thoughts, Change Your Life by Wayne W. Dyer

The Power of Intention by Wayne W. Dyer

The Seven Habits of Highly Effective People by Stephen Covey

The Richest Man in Babylon by George S. Clason

Awaken the Giant Within by Tony Robbins

A Course in Miracles by Helen Schucman

Good to Great by Jim Collins

Iacocca by Lee Iacocca

Getting Things Done by David Allen

Principles by Ray Dalio

The Trillion Dollar Coach by Eric Schmidt

Start with Why by Simon Sinek

Setting the Table by Danny Mayer